MAKING AUTHENTIC CRAFTSMAN FURNITURE

Instructions and Plans for 62 Projects

Articles from *The Craftsman*

edited by

GUSTAV STICKLEY

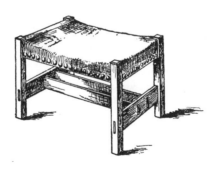

DOVER PUBLICATIONS, INC., NEW YORK

Published in Canada by General Publishing Company, Ltd., 30 Lesmill Road, Don Mills, Toronto, Ontario.
Published in the United Kingdom by Constable and Company, Ltd.

Making Authentic Craftsman Furniture: Instructions and Plans for 62 Projects, first published in 1986, is a selection of articles from *The Craftsman* magazine, edited by Gustav Stickley and published from 1901 to 1916. The articles reprinted here originally appeared in the following issues of *The Craftsman:* page 1, May 1905; pages 2–3, July 1903; pages 4–5, March 1905; pages 6–13, April 1905; pages 14–21, May 1905; pages 22–27, June 1905; pages 28–33, August 1905; pages 34–39, October 1905; pages 40–45, November 1905; pages 46–49, December 1905; pages 50–53, January 1906; pages 54–57, February 1906; pages 58–63, March 1906; pages 64–67, April 1906; pages 68–71, May 1906; pages 72–75, June 1906; pages 76–81, October 1906; pages 82–83, November 1906; pages 84–85, December 1906; pages 86–89, January 1907; pages 90–97, February 1907; pages 98–99, April 1907; pages 100–1, December 1906; pages 102–3, April 1907; pages 104–7, May 1907; pages 108–9, August 1905; pages 110–15, July 1907; pages 116–17, August 1907; pages 118–19, September 1907.

Manufactured in the United States of America
Dover Publications, Inc., 31 East 2nd Street, Mineola, N.Y. 11501

Library of Congress Cataloging in Publication Data
Main entry under title:

Making authentic craftsman furniture.

Articles from *The Craftsman*, edited by Gustav Stickley and published between 1901 and 1916.
1. Furniture making. I. Stickley, Gustav, 1858–1942. II. Craftsman (Albany, N.Y.)
TT194.M35 1986 684.1′04 85-13075
ISBN 0-486-25000-8 (pbk.)

Publisher's Note

This book contains instructions and plans for making sixty-two pieces of authentic Craftsman furniture. The projects are reprinted directly from Gustav Stickley's important magazine, *The Craftsman,* published from 1901 to 1916. Plans for furniture were a regular feature of *The Craftsman;* the projects reprinted here (with one exception) first appeared in the twenty-part series "Home Training in Cabinet Work," which ran in about two out of every three monthly issues between March 1905 and September 1907. (The series was followed by other, shorter series such as "Lessons in Practical Cabinet Work" and "Lessons in Practical Cabinetmaking and Metal Work.")

In addition to their intrinsic merit as pleasing and useful domestic objects, the pieces shown here exemplify a pivotal development in American decorative arts. Although related to the work of William Morris and the Arts and Crafts Movement in England, as witness the Morris chair included here, Stickley's publication developed a unique style. The simple, straightforward Craftsman approach to furniture— relatively unornamented pieces with clean, functional lines—became a classic American style in its own right. (For further information on Craftsman furniture, see *Stickley Craftsman Furniture Catalogs,* Dover 23838-5.)

Each project reprinted here generally includes the following: a brief statement of the item's character, including suggestions for appropriate varieties of wood; a "mill bill" giving complete lumber specifications; schematic drawings or diagrams of the piece, showing both front and side views with dimensions; a perspective drawing of the completed piece. An Index of Projects appears on page 121.

Contents

A FOOT REST

THIS piece of furniture is designed for a foot rest, but might find plenty of use in a house, especially in a bedroom, where it could be used for a slipper stool. Its construction needs no further explanation than is apparent from the drawing. The wood could well be one of the harder variety: oak, chestnut, mahogany or maple—either fumed or stained. The seat cover could be of leather or tapestry fastened with brass, copper or iron nails. For a section showing the method of upholstering, attention is called to the plans of the desk chair shown on page 15.

MILL BILL FOR FOOT REST

Pieces	No.	Long.	Rough Wide	Thick	Finish Wide	Thick
Legs	4	15 in.	2 in.	2 in.	1¾ in.	1¾ in.
Seat rails	2	20 in.	3 in.	1 in.	pattern	⅞ in.
Seat rails	2	15 in.	3 in.	1 in.	2¾ in.	⅞ in.
End stretchers	2	17 in.	3 in.	1 in.	2¾ in.	¾ in.
Center stretchers...	2	22 in.	1¾ in.	¾ in.	1½ in.	½ in.

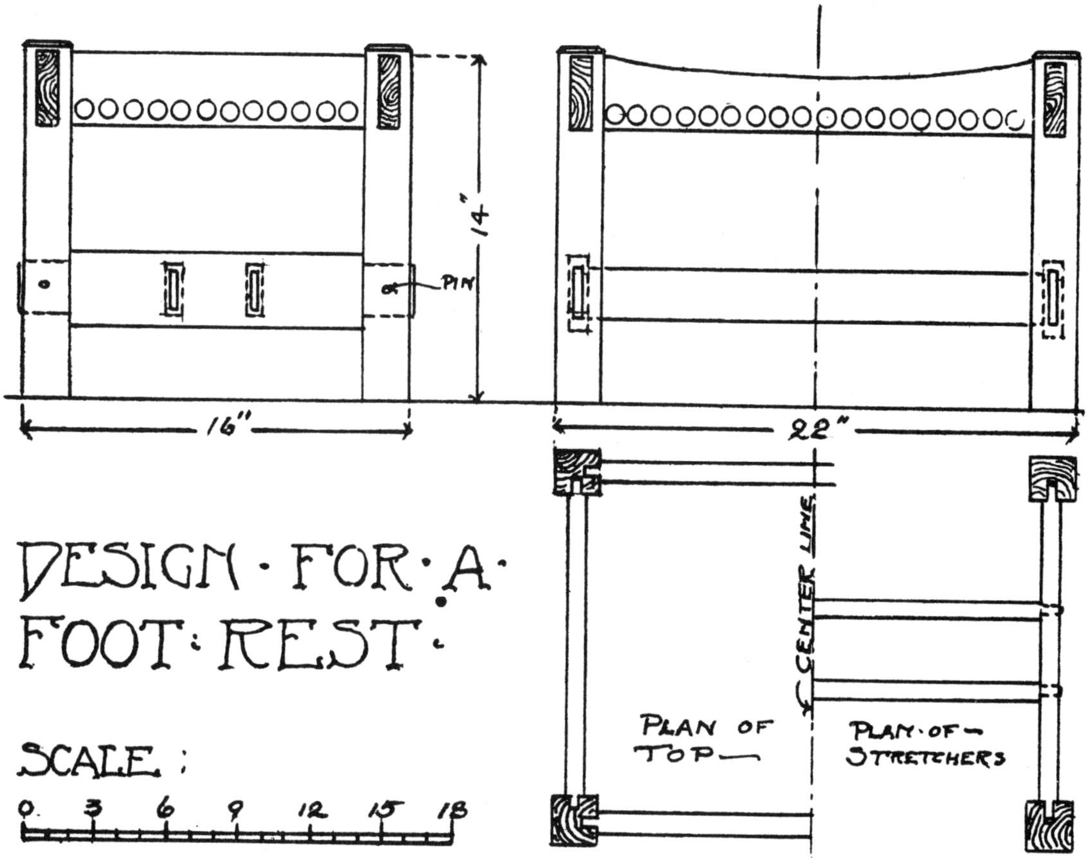

DESIGN · FOR · A · FOOT · REST ·

SCALE :

0   3   6   9   12   15   18

PIN

14"

16"

22"

CENTER LINE

PLAN OF TOP

PLAN · OF STRETCHERS

A Man's Dressing Cabinet

ONE seldom finds a more simple, convenient object of household use than the man's dressing cabinet here illustrated, which combines the functions usually filled by two or three pieces, by uniting them into a compact whole. The cabinet has the additional advantages of being pleasing in appearance, and so simple in construction that any craftsman may easily build it, in accordance with the subjoined directions.

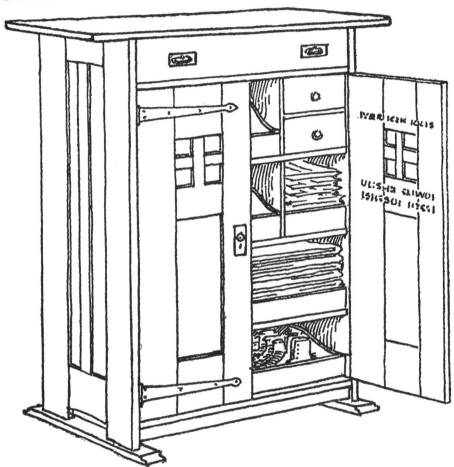

The dimensions of the piece are fifty-four inches in height by thirty-six inches wide and twenty-four inches deep, with a framing of seven-eighth inch stuff, as indicated, and with one-half inch panels. The doors are provided with strap-hinges, and, on the inside, are lettered with such inscriptions as may suit the fancy of the individual builder.

A Man's Dressing Cabinet

The large, topmost drawer, running the entire length of the piece, is five inches deep, and is designed for a general utility place. The small upper drawer at the right, is fitted, like a change-drawer, with six saucer-like divisions for shirt, collar, and sleeve buttons, and other small objects which are easily lost. Behind lies a space for handkerchiefs. This drawer, the one beneath it, and the two on the left are five inches deep.

The compartments in the center of the cabinet and those which are beneath the small lateral drawers pull out. Their dimensions are ten and one-half by ten inches.

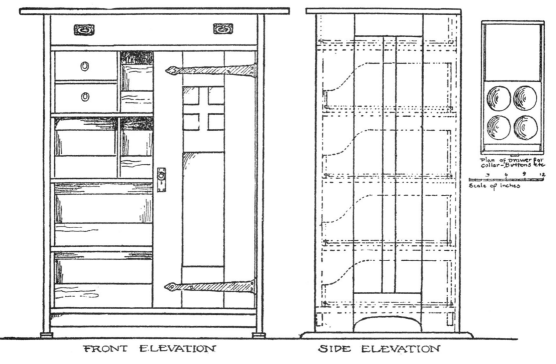

FRONT ELEVATION   SIDE ELEVATION

The two large trays at the bottom are used, the one for shoes, and the other for trousers. The space thus afforded, permits the garments to be laid aside without folding at the knee.

By this device, as well as by the other provisions of the cabinet, all folding and rumpling of clothing are obviated. Furthermore, when the doors are opened, the wardrobe lies ready for use: a saving of time which will be appreciated by the hard-working business or professional man of many engagements, for whom a minute saved is sometimes a fortune gained.

3

CHILD'S ARM CHAIR

IN building this chair put all together excepting the arms, and when the glue is dry the arm dowells are fitted and the back ones shoved into place; then, by pressure, the front will spring into its proper position. All dowells are well glued, and the glue is warmed before using. Attention is called also to the joining of the seat rails, also the three-eighths of an inch cut from the bottom of the back post after the chair is put together. This makes a little slant back to the seat, and gives a comfortable posi-

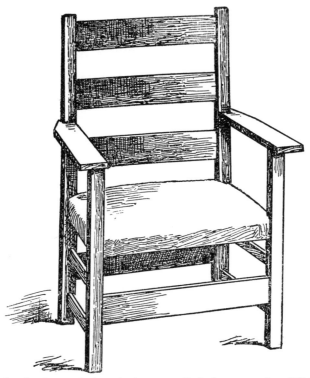

to the sitter. The back slats of the chairs are slightly curved. This is done by thoroughly wetting or steaming the wood and pressing it into shape—then allowing it to dry. The accompanying drawing will illustrate a device for this purpose, which for the amateur is quite as practical as a steam press.

MILL BILL OF LUMBER FOR CHILD'S ARM CHAIR

	Pieces	ROUGH			FINISH	
		Long	Wide	Thick	Wide	Thick
Front posts.....	2	18 in.	1½ in.	1½ in.	1¼ in.	1¼ in.
Back posts......	2	26 in.	2 in.	1½ in.	pattern	1¼ in.
Seat rails......	4	15 in.	1½ in.	1 in.	1¼ in.	¾ in.
F. & B. stretcher	2	15 in.	2½ in.	⅝ in.	2¼ in.	⅜ in.
Side stretcher...	4	13 in.	1¼ in.	⅝ in.	1 in.	⅜ in.
Back slats......	3	15 in.	2¼ in.	⅝ in.	2½ in.	⅜ in.
Arms	2	15 in.	2¾ in.	⅞ in.	2½ in.	⅝ in.

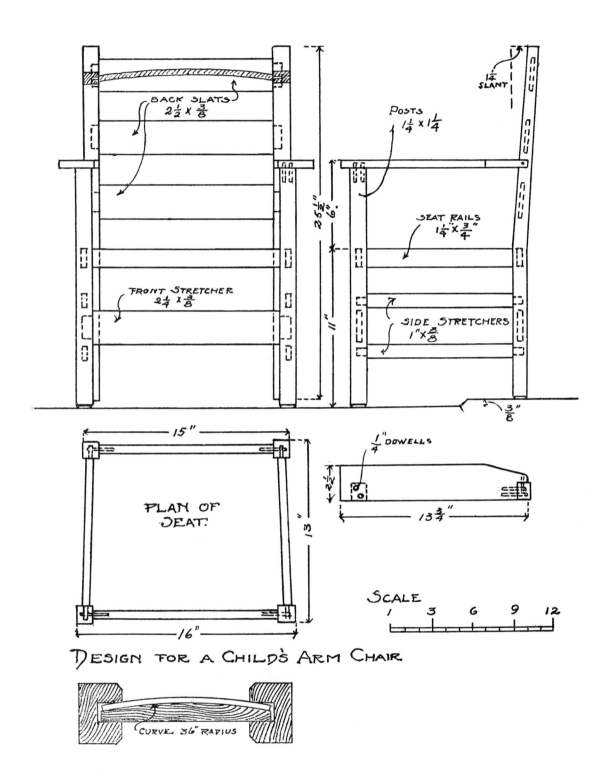

BACK SLATS
2½ x ⅜

POSTS
1¼ x 1¼

1¼
SLANT

SEAT RAILS
1¼" X ¾"

FRONT STRETCHER
2¼ X ⅜

SIDE STRETCHERS
1" X ⅜

25½"

6"

11"

⅜"

15"

¼" DOWELLS

2½"

13¾"

PLAN OF
SEAT.

13

16"

SCALE

1   3   6   9   12

DESIGN FOR A CHILD'S ARM CHAIR

CURVE 36" RADIUS

5

TWO DESIGNS FOR TABOURETS

THESE pieces are almost identical in construction, yet differ in size and shape of the top. Either one would be a useful addition to almost any room for the purpose of holding a jardiniere, while the larger one might be used as a small tea table.

A few construction points may be noted: Where the tenons of the legs come through the top they should be wedged—then planed flush with the top. In cutting the mortises for the stretchers of the square tabouret note that there is one-half an inch difference in the heights of the two stretchers. A dowel pin three-eights of an inch in diameter runs all the way through the legs holding the tenon of the stretcher—this is planed off flush with the sides of the leg.

Round Tabouret

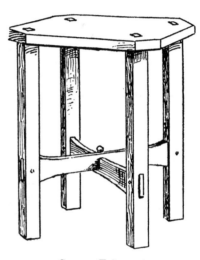

Square Tabouret

ROUND TABOURET—MILL BILL

	Pieces	Long	Rough Wide	Thick	Finish Wide	Thick
Top	1	17 in.	17 in.	1 in.	16 in. diam.	7/8 in.
Legs	4	19 in.	1½ in.	1½ in.	1⅜ in.	1⅜ in.
Stretchers	2	15 in.	2½ in.	¾ in.	pattern	⅝ in.

SQUARE TABOURET

	Pieces	Long	Wide	Thick	Wide	Thick
Top	1	18 in.	18 in.	1⅛ in.	17 in.	1 in.
Legs	4	23 in.	2 in.	2 in.	1¾ in.	1¾ in.
Stretchers	2	19 in.	2½ in.	1 in.	pattern	¾ in.

Any soft wood, as pine or white wood, may be used, or the harder woods, if desired.

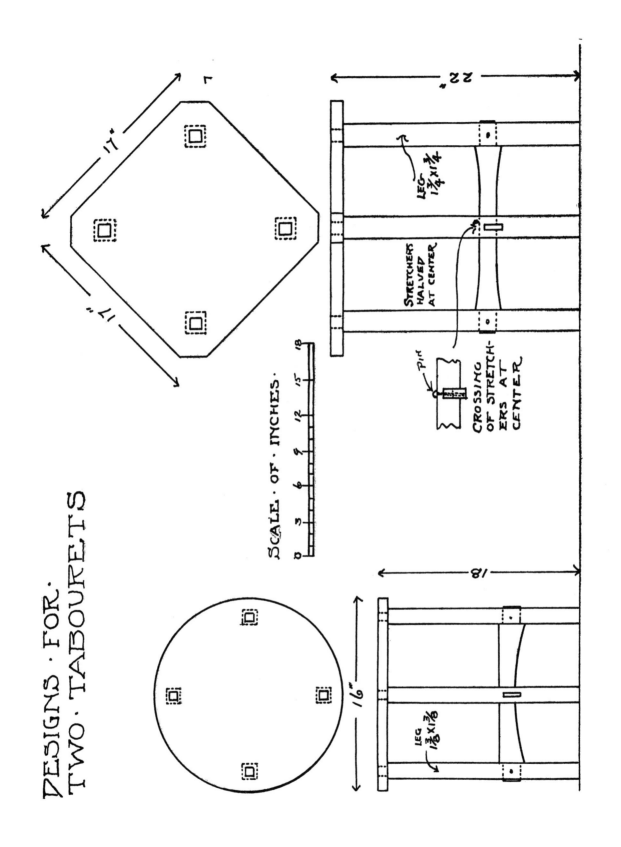

DESIGNS·FOR·
TWO·TABOURETS

SCALE · OF · INCHES ·

LEG- 1¾×1¾

STRETCHERS HALVED AT CENTER

PIN

CROSSING OF STRETCH- ERS AT CENTER

LEG 1⅜×1⅜

7

SMALL OCTAGONAL TABOURET

THIS table is rather a heavy one in design and could well be used for a den, living room, library or man's room. The legs slanting outward give it a sturdy appearance. It could be used as a jardiniere stand, to hold a cigar-box and ash tray, or on a hot day a place to rest a tray with cool drinks.

Little needs to be said concerning its construction, as what has already been said about the preceding tables covers this one with possibly the exception of the stretcher keys—these must not be driven so hard as to split the wood which there is some danger of doing at the end of the tenons.

Octagonal Tabouret

SMALL TABLE, OCTAGONAL TOP—MILL BILL

	Pieces	Long	Rough Wide	Thick	Finish Wide	Thick
Top	1	23 in.	23 in.	1⅛ in.	22 in.	1 in.
Legs	4	22 in.	6½ in.	1 in.	6 in.	⅞ in.
Stretchers	2	25 in.	3½ in.	1 in.	3 in.	⅞ in.
Keys	4	4 in.	1 in.	1 in.	¾ in.	⅝ in.
Top braces......	2	20 in.	2½ in.	1 in.	2 in.	⅞ in.

Any soft wood, as pine or white wood, may be used, or the harder woods, if desired.

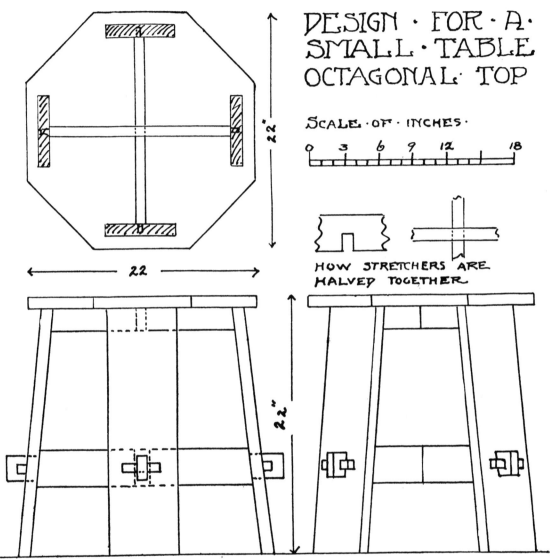

DESIGN · FOR · A·
SMALL · TABLE
OCTAGONAL · TOP

SCALE · OF · INCHES ·

0   3   6   9   12   18

HOW STRETCHERS ARE
HALVED TOGETHER

22

22"

22

22"

Tabouret or Table with Octagonal Top

9

ROUND TABLE

THIS piece is designed for use in a room where a light treatment is carried out and would make a good bedroom or sewing room table and might possibly find its place, for occasional use, in a living room.

The construction is very simple and little need be said except that all the joints should be well made so the table will be rigid—especially the brace under the top which keeps the piece firm. The top is fastened on with "table irons." A full-sized sketch is here given—these irons are first screwed to the top braces—then the work is turned up-side-down and the screws put in which fasten the top to the base.

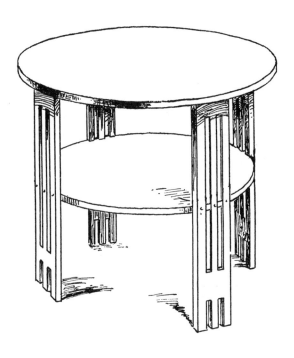

ROUND TABLE—MILL BILL

	Pieces	Long	ROUGH Wide	Thick	FINISH Wide	Thick
Top	1	36 in.	36 in.	1⅛ in.	36 in. diam.	1 in.
Shelf	1	28 in.	28 in.	1 in.	28 in. diam.	⅞ in.
Legs	4	30 in.	6½ in.	1¼ in.	6 in.	1⅛ in.
Top braces......	2	37 in.	3 in.	1 in.	2½ in.	⅞ in.

Use oak, chestnut, mahogany, or any medium hard wood.

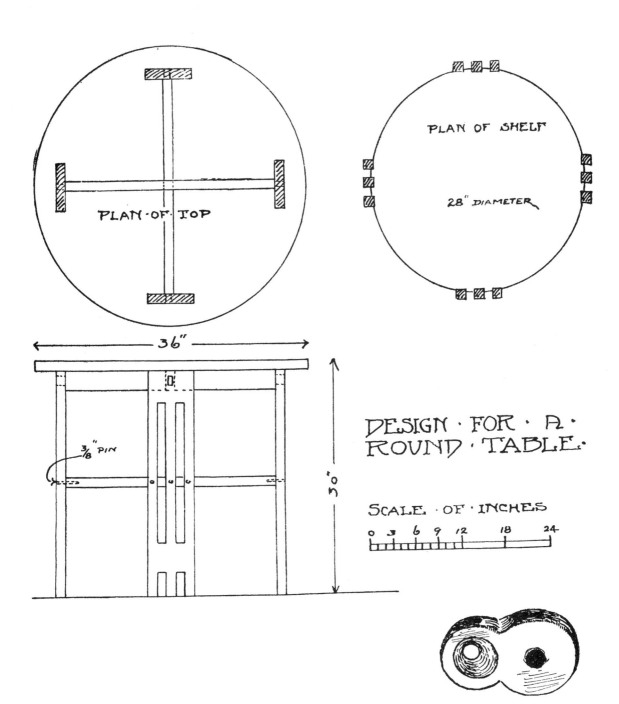

PLAN·OF·TOP

PLAN OF SHELF

28" DIAMETER

36"

3/8" PIN

30"

DESIGN · FOR · A ·
ROUND · TABLE ·

SCALE · OF · INCHES

0   3   6   9   12   18   24

Table Iron

THE DROP-LEAF TABLE

THIS is a table suited to many uses. Its top when opened, is forty inches square—quite large enough to be used as a breakfast table, and for a living room. Its chief advantage is that when the leaves are dropped the space occupied by it is very small, so that it can be moved back out of the way against the wall. A little clever handling of the wood will be needed to make a good joint where the leaves join the top, and careful attention is called to the enlarged detail shown on the plans—also note that the wood needs to be taken out the width of the hinge to allow for the eye of the hinge—these should be two inches wide and placed about four inches from the ends, secured with plenty of screws:

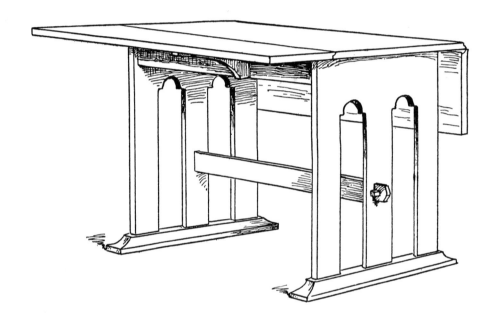

DROP-LEAF TABLE—MILL BILL

	Pieces	Long	Rough Wide	Thick	Finish Wide	Thick
Top	1	41 in.	20½ in.	1⅛ in.	20 in.	1 in.
Leaves	2	41 in.	11¼ in.	1⅛ in.	10¾ in.	1 in.
Ends	2	30 in.	16½ in.	1¼ in.	16 in.	1⅛ in.
Bottom brace.....	2	22 in.	3½ in.	2¼ in.	3 in.	2 in.
Table rails.......	2	30 in.	4½ in.	1 in.	4 in.	⅞ in.
Stretcher	1	34 in.	3½ in.	1¼ in.	3 in.	1⅛ in.
Leaf bracket.....	2	12 in.	3½ in.	1¼ in.	pattern	1⅛ in.

Use oak, cherry, maple, or one of the hard woods.

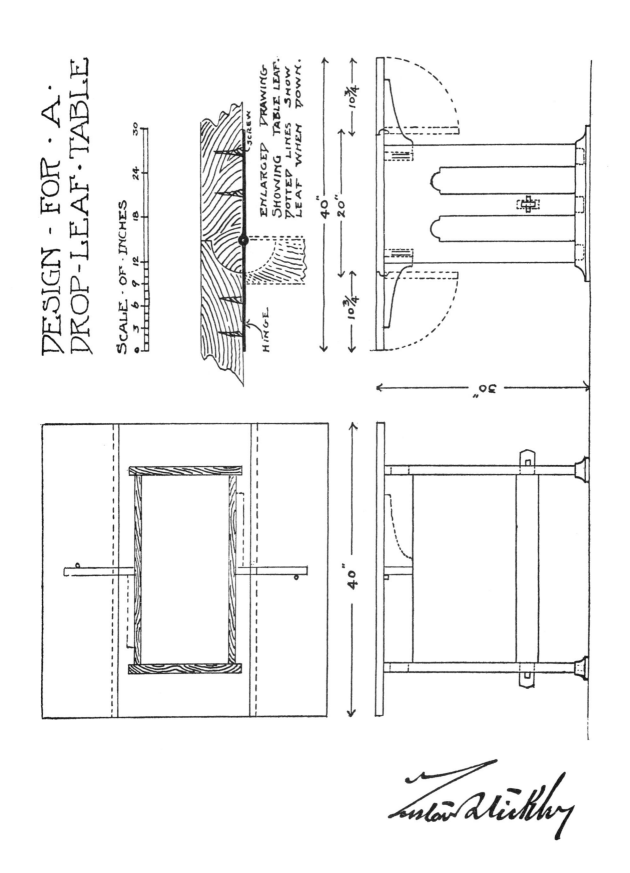

DESIGN · FOR · A ·
DROP · LEAF · TABLE

SCALE · OF · INCHES

ENLARGED · DRAWING ·
SHOWING · TABLE · LEAF ·
DOTTED · LINES · SHOW ·
LEAF · WHEN · DOWN ·

SCREW

HINGE

40"

20"

10¾

10¾

30"

40"

13

DESK CHAIR

IN building a chair the sides are put together separately and then the front and back rails and stretchers last, the side seat rails being mortised and tenoned, the front and back seat rails are dowelled, thereby pinning the tenons. The slight difference in the length of the front and back legs gives a comfortable slant to the seat. The back slats are curved, which is done by thoroughly soaking the wood with water, or better, steaming it and then pressing it into shape and allowing it to dry in the little press which is shown herewith.

CURVE 36" RADIUS

MILL BILL FOR A DESK CHAIR

Pieces	No.	Long	ROUGH Wide	Thick	FINISH Wide	Thick
Front posts	2	18 in.	1⅜ in.	1⅜ in.	1¼ in.	1¼ in.
Back posts	2	31 in.	2½ in.	1⅜ in.	pattern	1¼ in.
Seat rails	4	15 in.	1½ in.	1 in.	1¼ in.	¾ in.
F. & B. stretchers..	2	15 in.	3¼ in.	½ in.	3 in.	⅜ in.
Side stretchers	4	15 in.	1⅜ in.	½ in.	1¼ in.	⅜ in.
Back slat	1	15 in.	6¼ in.	½ in.	6 in.	⅜ in.

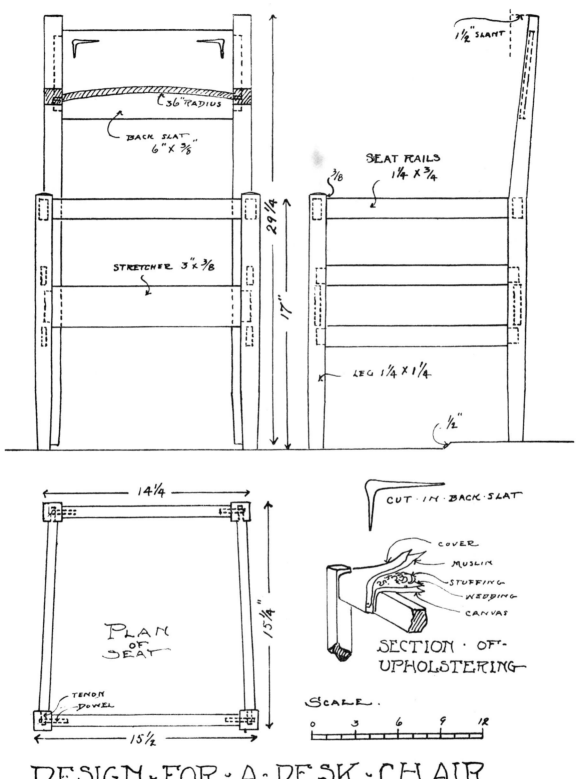

1½" SLANT

36" RADIUS

BACK SLAT
6" X ⅜"

SEAT RAILS
1¼ X ¾

⅜

29¼

17"

STRETCHER 3" X ⅜

LEG 1¼ X 1¼

½"

14¼

15¼"

PLAN
OF
SEAT

TENON
DOWEL

15½

CUT IN BACK SLAT

COVER
MUSLIN
STUFFING
WEDDING
CANVAS

SECTION · OF·
UPHOLSTERING

SCALE.

0   3   6   9   12

DESIGN·FOR·A·DESK·CHAIR

SCREEN

A GOOD screen is one of the very useful things which go toward the furnishing of a house. The one given herewith is of such a size that it is convenient for general use and not so heavy as to be hard to move about from room to room wherever it may be needed. The wood of which it is made may vary, but we will suppose it is made of poplar, a light weight wood, and stained gray-green. The fabric part of the screen may be inexpensive or of medium price as, for instance, a Japanese silk of a green tone just a little darker than the wood stain, a quiet color effect which would harmonize with almost any color scheme.

The curtain hangs on quarter inch solid brass rods at top and bottom. Care will need to be taken in cutting and fitting the dovetails which project one-sixteenth of an inch beyond the face of the panel. The panels being V-jointed and splined gives them a chance to shrink and swell without making ugly looking cracks.

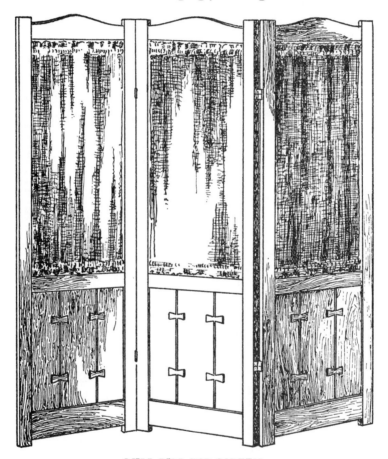

MILL BILL FOR SCREEN

Pieces	No.	Rough			Finish	
		Long	Wide	Thick	Wide	Thick
Sides	6	61 in.	2½ in.	1⅛ in.	2¼ in.	1 in.
Tops	3	18 in.	4 in.	1⅛ in.	pattern	1 in.
Center rail	3	18 in.	2½ in.	1⅛ in.	2¼ in.	1 in.
Lower rail	3	18 in.	4½ in.	1⅛ in.	4 in.	1 in.
Panels	6	18 in.	5½ in.	¾ in.	5 in.	½ in.
Panels	3	18 in.	6¾ in.	¾ in.	6½ in.	½ in.
Dove-tail	1	9 in.	9 in.	1 in.	pattern	⅞ in.

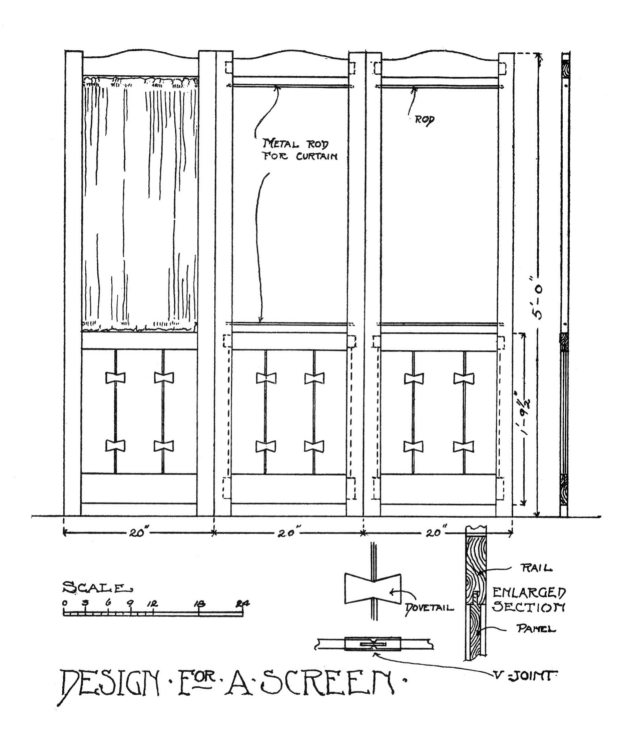

METAL ROD
FOR CURTAIN

ROD

5'-0"

1'-9½"

20" · 20" · 20"

SCALE
0   3   6   9   12   18   24

DOVETAIL

RAIL
ENLARGED
SECTION
PANEL

V-JOINT

DESIGN · FOR · A · SCREEN ·

17

SHIRT-WAIST BOX

THIS piece of furniture is one that would take the place of the ordinary chintz-covered cracker-box which, placed under a window, makes a convenient window-seat. If the tray were left out it could be used as a hall chest and a place to keep overshoes. Here it would be made of oak and its top covered with leather fastened by brass or copper nails.

The top is made firm by two strips running across the ends into which the center portion is tongued. The till is simply a box without any bottom and around the lower edge is tacked a piece of light weight canvas. This makes all the bottom necessary and adds much to the lightness of the tray. Small loops of canvas, by which it can be lifted, are tacked to the ends.

MILL BILL FOR SHIRT-WAIST BOX

Pieces	No.	Rough Long	Rough Wide	Thick	Finish Wide	Thick
Center of top	1	33 in.	18½ in.	1 in.	18 in.	⅞ in.
Ends of top	2	19 in.	6¾ in.	1 in.	6½ in.	⅞ in.
Front and back stiles	4	16 in.	6½ in.	1⅛ in.	6 in.	1 in.
End stiles	4	16 in.	..	1⅛ in.	..	1 in.
Top and bot. rails	4	34 in.	4½ in.	1⅛ in.	4 in.	1 in.
Center stile	2	10 in.	6½ in.	1⅛ in.	6 in.	1 in.
Panels	4	14 in.	8½ in.	¾ in.	8 in.	½ in.
End panels	2	8 in.	8½ in.	¾ in.	8 in.	½ in.
Bottom	1	41 in.	16 in.	¾ in.	15½ in.	½ in.
Tray sides	2	41 in.	4½ in.	½ in.	4 in.	⅜ in.
Tray ends	2	16 in.	4½ in.	½ in.	4 in.	⅜ in.
Lineal feet strips	9	..	1 in.	¾ in.	¾ in.	½ in.

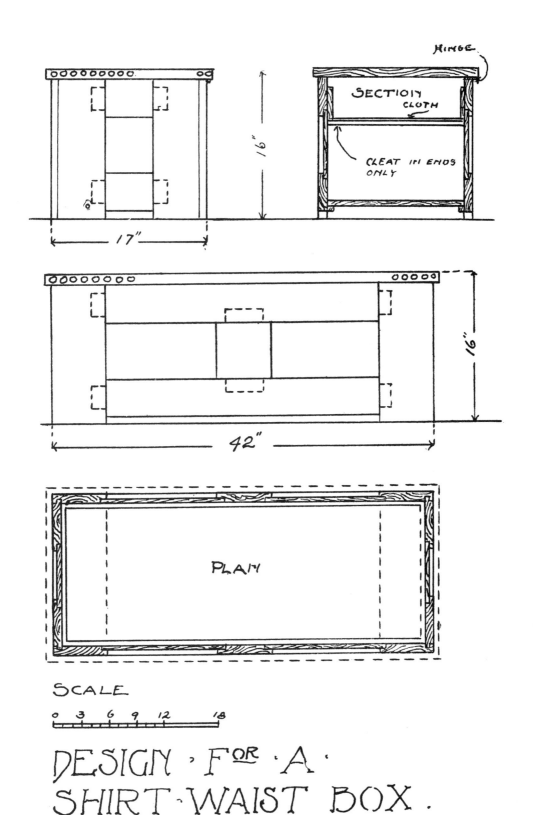

HINGE

SECTION
CLOTH

CLEAT IN ENDS
ONLY

16"

17"

16"

42"

PLAN

SCALE

0   3   6   9   12   18

DESIGN · FOR · A ·
SHIRT · WAIST · BOX.

GARDEN BENCH

THIS garden bench is made of white cedar stock stripped of the bark and left in the natural color which in time takes a silver gray tone and a beautiful texture. The seat rails, back and arms are smoothly planed so that no rough, disturbing places are left. Each piece will need to be fitted with care, as after the tenon and mortise are cut the entire stick must be slightly set into the piece to which it is joined. This prevents the water from getting into the joint and makes a workmanlike job. A chair can easily be made from these plans by making the front and back rails twenty-six inches in length and using only eight rails for the seat.

MILL BILL FOR GARDEN BENCH

Pieces	No.	Long	Thick	
Front posts	2	29 in.	3½ in. diameter	round
Back posts	2	39 in.	3½ in. diameter	round
Top of back	1	64 in.	3 in. diameter	½ in. round
Front and back seat rail	2	64 in.	3 in. diameter	¾ in. round
Back slats	9	15 in.	2½ in. diameter	½ in. round
Arms	2	24 in.	5 in. diameter	2½ in. thick
End seat rails	2	21 in.	3 in. diameter	¾ in. round
Seat rails	20	21 in.	2½ in. diameter	½ in. round
End stretchers	2	25 in.	3 in. diameter	round

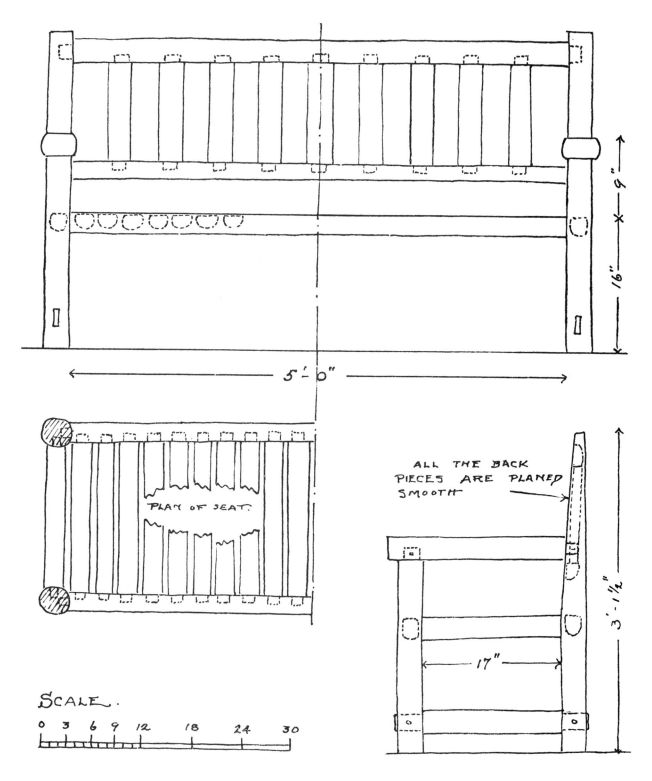

16" x 9"

5'-0"

PLAN OF SEAT.

ALL THE BACK
PIECES ARE PLANED
SMOOTH

3'-1½"

17"

SCALE.

0   3   6 9 12   18   24   30

DESIGN · FOR · A · GARDEN · BENCH ·

THIS is a useful piece in any living room where loose papers and magazines are apt to accumulate. The purpose in making it larger at the bottom is to attain greater symmetry and to give the idea of stability. A perfectly vertical stand would appear narrower at the bottom than at the top.

Put together the entire end first, then the shelves, the top and bottom ones, however, being last. Do not drive the keys in tenon holes hard enough to split the wood. Note that the three center shelves are slightly let in at full size into the posts and end uprights.

As such a stand may need to be moved, it is appropriate that it be made of soft wood if desirable. Whether of hard or soft wood it should be suitably colored.

MILL BILL FOR MAGAZINE CABINET

Pieces	No.	Long	Rough Wide	Thick	Finish Wide	Thick
Posts	4	44 in.	2½ in.	1⅜ in.	2 in.	1¼ in.
Top of end.......	2	9 in.	5¼ in.	1¼ in.	5 in.	1⅛ in.
Base of end.......	2	12 in.	5¼ in.	1¼ in.	5 in.	1⅛ in.
Top	1	19 in.	9¼ in.	1¼ in.	9 in.	1 in.
Bottom	1	19 in.	11¼ in.	1¼ in.	11 in.	1 in.
Shelves	3	14 in.	10¾ in.	1 in.	10½ in.	¾ in.
Keys	1	4 in.	5 in.	1 in.	pattern	¾ in.
End ballusters	6	48 in.	1⅛ in.	1⅛ in.	1 in.	1 in.

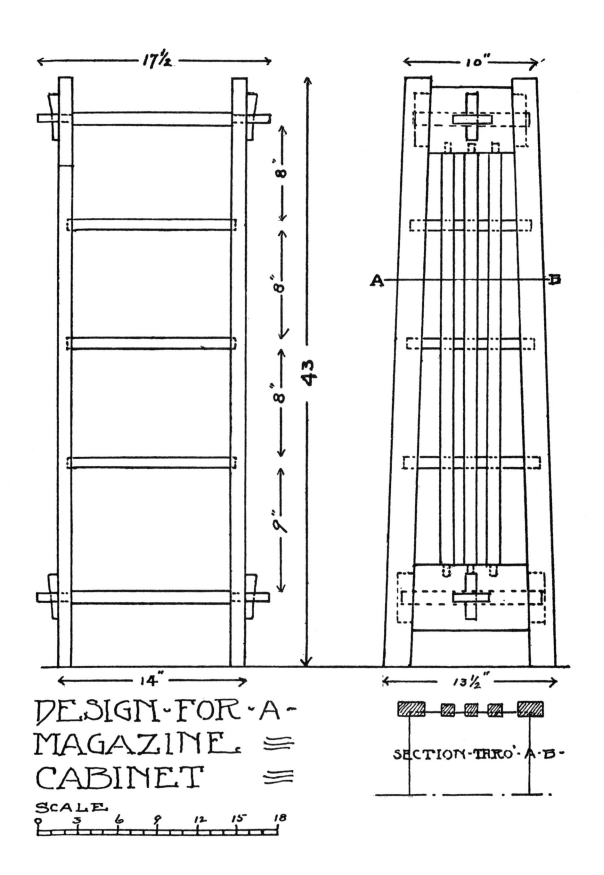

17½

8"
8"
8"
9"
43

14"

10"

A———B

13½"

DESIGN·FOR·A·
MAGAZINE·
CABINET

SECTION·THRO'·A·B·

SCALE
0   3   6   9   12   15   18

LIBRARY TABLE

THIS useful piece is of good size, having a top thirty-two by fifty-four inches. Instead of having a shelf underneath, a series of slats, placed at a slight distance apart, is introduced. In building it, put the ends together first. The sides of the drawers are dovetailed, and each drawer has a stop underneath it to keep it from going in too far. This stop should hold the face of the drawer one-sixteenth of an inch back of the front rail. The practical reason for this is that, should the piece shrink in any degree, the unevenness is less likely to show when the drawer is thus slightly recessed. Bevel off the lower edges of the legs to prevent tearing the carpet, and carefully sandpaper the edges of the top to remove the sharpness. Oak is the best material of which to construct this table, as it is needed to be substantial, strong and firm. The pulls are of copper or iron, hammered preferably, yet any good pulls will serve admirably.

MILL BILL FOR LIBRARY TABLE

Pieces	No.	Long	Rough Wide	Thick	Finish Wide	Thick
Top	1	55 in.	33 in.	1¼ in.	32 in.	1⅛ in.
Legs	4	30 in.	2⅞ in.	2⅞ in.	2¾ in.	2¾ in.
End stretcher	2	28 in.	3¾ in.	1⅜ in.	3½ in.	1¼ in.
End uprights	18	15 in.	1¼ in.	1 in.	1 in.	¾ in.
Shelf slats	9	45 in.	1¼ in.	1 in.	1 in.	¾ in.
End rail	2	28 in.	5¼ in.	1⅜ in.	5 in.	1¼ in.
Back rail	1	45 in.	5¼ in.	1 in.	5 in.	⅞ in.
Front rail	1	45 in.	2¾ in.	1 in.	2½ in.	⅞ in.
Division rails	3	7 in.	1½ in.	1 in.	1¼ in.	⅞ in.
Ledger rails	4	28 in.	1½ in.	1 in.	1¼ in.	⅞ in.
Drawer fronts	2	19 in.	5¼ in.	1 in.	5 in.	⅞ in.
Drawer Backs	2	19 in.	5¼ in.	¾ in.	5 in.	½ in.
Drawer sides	4	27 in.	5¼ in.	¾ in.	5 in.	½ in.
Drawer bottoms ..	2	19 in.	27½ in.	¾ in.	27 in.	½ in.

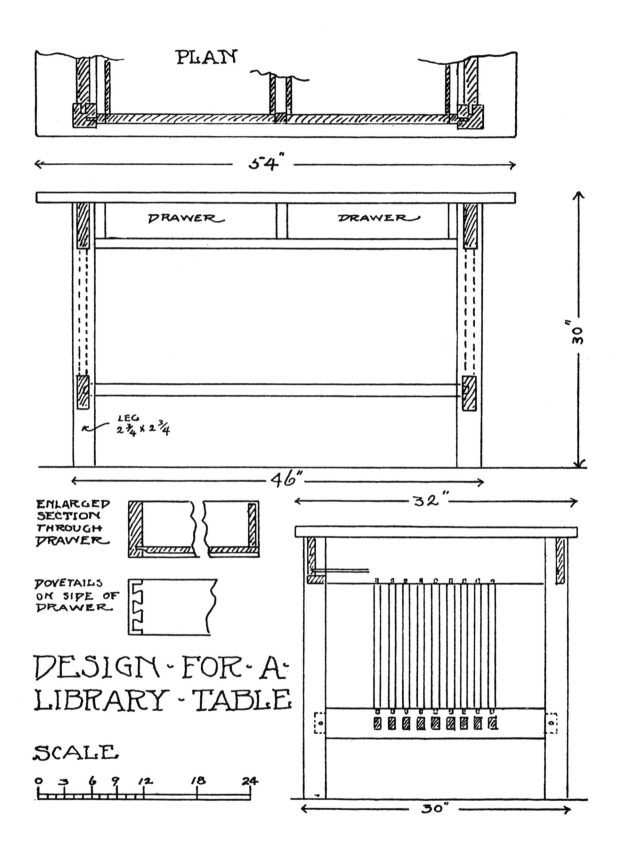

PLAN

5'4"

DRAWER   DRAWER

30"

LEG
2¾ x 2¾

46"

32"

ENLARGED
SECTION
THROUGH
DRAWER

DOVETAILS
ON SIDE OF
DRAWER

DESIGN·FOR·A·
LIBRARY·TABLE

SCALE

0   3   6   9   12   18   24

30"

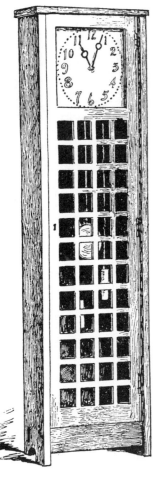

HALL CLOCK

THIS simple, yet almost necessary piece in a well equipped house, is made of oak, mahogany or other suitable hard wood. It is six feet high, with a door the whole size of the front. The upper part is a glass panel and the lower is filled with square panes. Small butt hinges are used for the door, and it is made so as to lock.

The face is made of wood with the figures burned on, or of metal. If preferred the enameled zinc or tin face usually supplied with the clock movements may be used, though we like the wood or metal better. The face is twelve inches square. If the case is made of mahogany, a brass face is most appropriate; if of oak, a copper face. If a wooden face is used it should be of a light colored wood with fine grain, such as holly or orange.

MILL BILL FOR CLOCK

Pieces	No.	Long	ROUGH Wide	Thick	FINISH Wide	Thick
Sides	2	72 in.	10½ in.	1⅜ in.	10 in.	1¼ in.
Top	1	23 in.	11 in.	1⅜ in.	10¾ in.	1¼ in.
Bottom rails	2	23 in.	4½ in.	1¼ in.	4 in.	1 in.
Door stiles	2	66 in.	2⅛ in.	1 in.	1⅞ in.	⅞ in.
Door rails	2	15 in.	2½ in.	1 in.	2 in.	⅞ in.
Lower door rail	1	15 in.	3½ in.	1 in.	3 in.	⅞ in.
Door mullions	3	47 in.	1¼ in.	1 in.	1 in.	⅞ in.
Door mullions	11	15 in.	1¼ in.	1 in.	1 in.	⅞ in.
Back stiles	2	50 in.	3 in.	1 in.	2½ in.	¾ in.
Back rails	2	18 in.	6½ in.	1 in.	6 in.	¾ in.
Back panel	1	44 in.	14½ in.	¾ in.	14 in.	½ in.
Bottom	1	19 in.	8½ in.	1 in.	8 in.	⅞ in.
Back door stiles	4	19 in.	2¾ in.	1 in.	2½ in.	¾ in.
Back door panel	1	14 in.	14½ in.	¾ in.	14 in.	½ in.
Movement shelf	1	19 in.	5½ in.	1 in.	5 in.	⅞ in.
Stops	2	72 in.	1½ in.	¾ in.	1¼ in.	½ in.

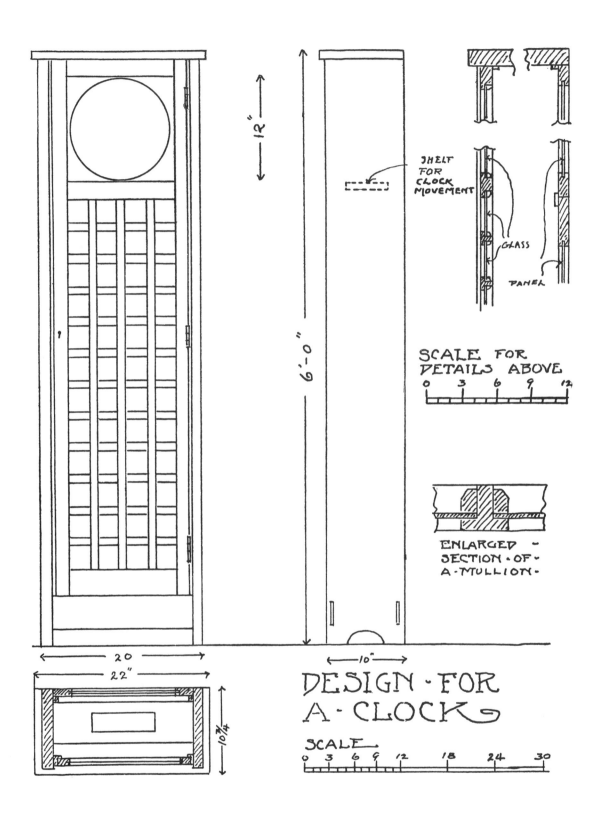

12"

6'-0"

SHELF
FOR
CLOCK
MOVEMENT

GLASS

PANEL

SCALE FOR
DETAILS ABOVE

0   3   6   9   12

ENLARGED -
SECTION · OF ·
A · MULLION ·

20

22"

10¾"

10"

DESIGN · FOR
A · CLOCK

SCALE

0   3   6   9   12   18   24   30

27

DINING TABLE

THE lines and proportions of this dining table are especially good. The octagonal legs and the graceful curve of the central braces give the piece a distinct style. The top is removable, having the braces which keep it from warping dove-tailed in and only fastened with a screw at the center, no glue being used, so that the top can shrink or swell slightly without doing any harm whatever. The mortise and tenon construction is used throughout with the exception of these dove-tailed top braces and the central shaped braces, which are secured by strong five-eighths inch dowels. When put together all the corners should be carefully taken off with a scraper and well sanded and then the finish applied. This table would be a suitable one to be used in a large living room or library, although it has the name of dining table attached to it.

MILL BILL FOR DINING TABLE

Pieces	No.	Long	Rough Wide	Rough Thick	Finish Wide	Finish Thick
Top	1	85 in.	42½ in.	1½ in.	42 in.	1⅜ in.
Legs	4	28 in.	4¼ in.	4¼ in.	4 in.	4 in.
Lower brace	2	36 in.	4½ in.	3¾ in.	4¼ in.	3½ in.
Upper brace	2	36 in.	4¼ in.	4 in.	4 in.	3¾ in.
Lower stretcher	1	66 in.	3¾ in.	3¾ in.	3½ in.	3½ in.
Upper stretcher	2	66 in.	2¼ in.	2 in.	2 in.	1¾ in.
Top braces	4	43 in.	3 in.	3 in.	2¾ in.	2¾ in.
Top center stretcher	1	20 in.	5¼ in.	2¼ in.	5 in.	2 in.
Shaped stretchers	2	36 in.	7 in.	2¾ in.	pattern	2½ in.

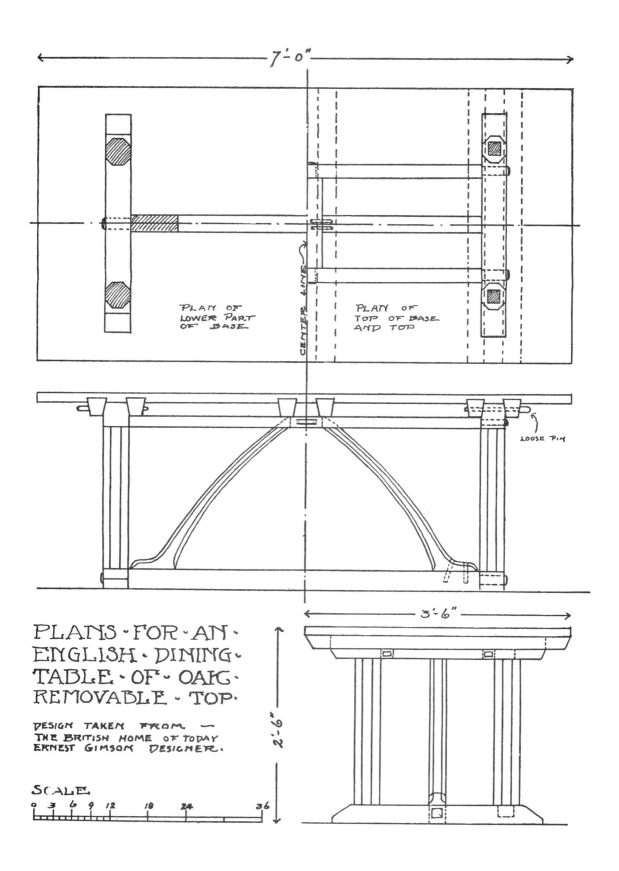

7'-0"

PLAN OF
LOWER PART
OF BASE

PLAN OF
TOP OF BASE
AND TOP

CENTER LINE

LOOSE PIN

PLANS · FOR · AN ·
ENGLISH · DINING ·
TABLE · OF · OAK ·
REMOVABLE · TOP.

DESIGN TAKEN FROM —
THE BRITISH HOME OF TODAY
ERNEST GIMSON DESIGNER.

SCALE.
0 3 6 9 12   18   24   36

3'-6"

2'-6"

ARM CHAIR

W HAT has been said concerning the construction of chairs in previous numbers[*] will apply to the work on this piece—as no new or unusual features appear unless it be in the back post, which is slanted on the outside, giving the chair an added quaintness. The seat and back are covered with heavy leather which must be stretched on when wet, and fastened with small headed tacks, care being taken to place the tacks so that the large heads of the ornamental nails will cover them. The leather must be allowed to dry thoroughly before the edge is trimmed.

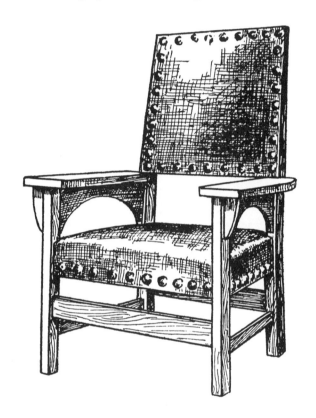

MILL BILL FOR ARM CHAIR

Pieces	No.	Long	Rough Wide	Rough Thick	Finish Wide	Finish Thick
Front post	2	27 in.	2 in.	2 in.	1¾ in.	1¾ in.
Back post	2	46 in.	2 in.	3 in.	1¾ in.	pattern
Seat rails	4	21 in.	4 in.	1 in.	3½ in.	⅞ in.
F. and B. stretcher	2	21 in.	3 in.	1 in.	2¾ in.	¾ in.
Side stretcher	2	20 in.	2 in.	1 in.	1¾ in.	¾ in.
Back rails	2	20 in.	2¾ in.	1 in.	2½ in.	⅞ in.
Arm	2	24 in.	4¾ in.	1⅛ in.	4½ in.	1 in.
Bracket	2	6 in.	2 in.	1½ in.	pattern	1¼ in.
Under arm	2	19 in.	7 in.	1 in.	pattern	1¼ in.

*See pages 4 and 14 of this edition.

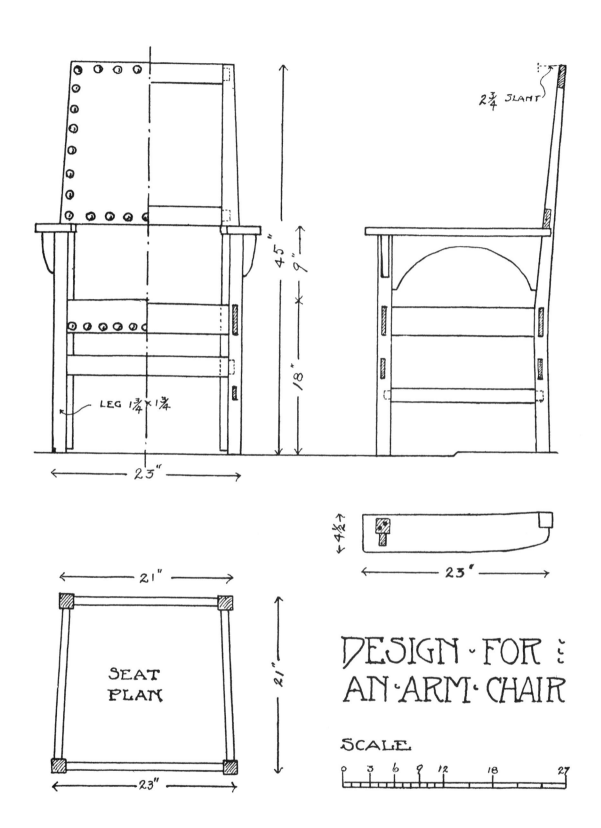

2¾ SLANT

45"

9"

18"

LEG 1¾ × 1¾

23"

4½

23'

21"

SEAT
PLAN

21"

23"

DESIGN · FOR ·
AN · ARM · CHAIR

SCALE

0   3   6   9   12   18   27

WRITING DESK

THIS writing desk is a piece of cabinet work which will depend, for its good appearance, upon well selected wood and good work, the entire face of the piece being flush—a single line out of true would mar the effect of the whole. The dove-tailing at the top and the shelf mortised through the sides at the bottom gives a firm and structural appearance. The slides, upon which the lid rests when down, have a small pin at about three inches from the back which stops the slide from pulling too far out. The doors and lid are cross veneered so that warping and shrinking are, to an extent, overcome. The hardware should be inconspicuous so that the beauty of wood grain and the simple lines will be accentuated.

MILL BILL FOR WRITING DESK

Pieces	No.	Long	Rough Wide	Thick	Finish Wide	Thick	Wood
Sides	2	48 in.	14¼ in.	1 in.	14 in.	¾ in.	oak
Top, bottom, shelf	3	31 in.	14¼ in.	1 in.	14 in.	¾ in.	oak
Lower rail	1	31 in.	2¾ in.	1 in.	2½ in.	⅞ in.	oak
Lid	1	30 in.	18¼ in.	1 in.	18 in.	¾ in.	oak
Veneer for lid	2	19 in.	30½ in.	$\frac{1}{16}$ in.	..	..	oak
Lower doors	2	18 in.	14¼ in.	1 in.	14 in.	¾ in.	oak
Division rail	1	18 in.	2 in.	1¼ in.	1¾ in.	1⅛ in.	oak
Partition	1	18 in.	14¼ in.	1 in.	14 in.	¾ in.	oak
Slide and division	2	15 in.	4¼ in.	1 in.	4 in.	¾ in.	oak
Drawer front	1	26 in.	4¼ in.	1 in.	4 in.	⅞ in.	oak
Drawer sides	2	15 in.	4¼ in.	¾ in.	4 in.	½ in.	oak
Drawer back	1	26 in.	4 in.	¾ in.	3¾ in.	½ in.	oak
Drawer bottom	1	26 in.	15 in.	½ in.	14¾ in.	⅜ in.	oak
Dust panel	1	26 in.	11¼ in.	½ in.	11 in.	⅜ in.	oak
Shelf	1	29 in.	11¼ in.	1 in.	11 in.	¾ in.	oak
Interior	12 running feet	10 in.	$\frac{3}{16}$ in.	..	⅛ in.		red cedar
Drawer front	1	11 in.	3 in.	¾ in.	2¾ in.	½ in.	red cedar
11 running feet			10 in.	$\frac{5}{16}$ in.	..	¼ in.	red cedar

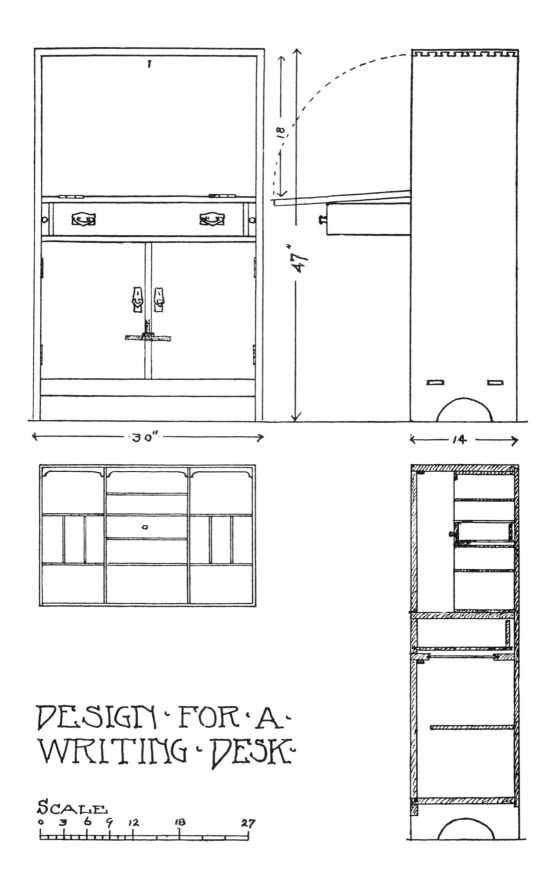

DESIGN · FOR · A ·
WRITING · DESK ·

SCALE
0   3   6   9   12   18   27

A BOOKCASE

THIS piece is designed to hold things as well as books. The top is fastned in place by half inch dowels placed not farther than three inches apart. The shelves are tenoned and the sides rabbited to within one and one-half inches of the front to receive them. The construction of the lattice as shown on the plans is as follows: The 3-16 inch stock for the face is halved at the intersecting points and on the backs are glued the 3-16 inch x 5-16 inch strips.

MILL BILL FOR BOOKCASE

Pieces	No.	Long	Rough Wide	Thick	Finish Wide	Thick
Sides	2	62 in.	$14\frac{1}{2}$ in.	$1\frac{1}{4}$ in.	14 in.	$1\frac{1}{8}$ in.
Top	1	62 in.	$14\frac{1}{2}$ in.	$1\frac{1}{4}$ in.	14 in.	$1\frac{1}{8}$ in.
Back	12	62 in.	$5\frac{1}{2}$ in.	1 in.	5 in.	$\frac{3}{4}$ in.
Shelves	3	62 in.	$13\frac{1}{2}$ in.	1 in.	13 in.	$\frac{3}{4}$ in.
Shelves	4	22 in.	12 in.	1 in.	11 in.	$\frac{3}{4}$ in.
Drawer rails	3	18 in.	14 in.	1 in.	13 in.	$\frac{3}{4}$ in.
Base strip	2	62 in.	2 in.	1 in.	$1\frac{3}{4}$ in.	$\frac{7}{8}$ in.
Partitions	2	30 in.	14 in.	1 in.	$13\frac{1}{2}$ in.	$\frac{3}{4}$ in.
Door stiles	4	30 in.	3 in.	1 in.	$2\frac{1}{2}$ in.	$\frac{7}{8}$ in.

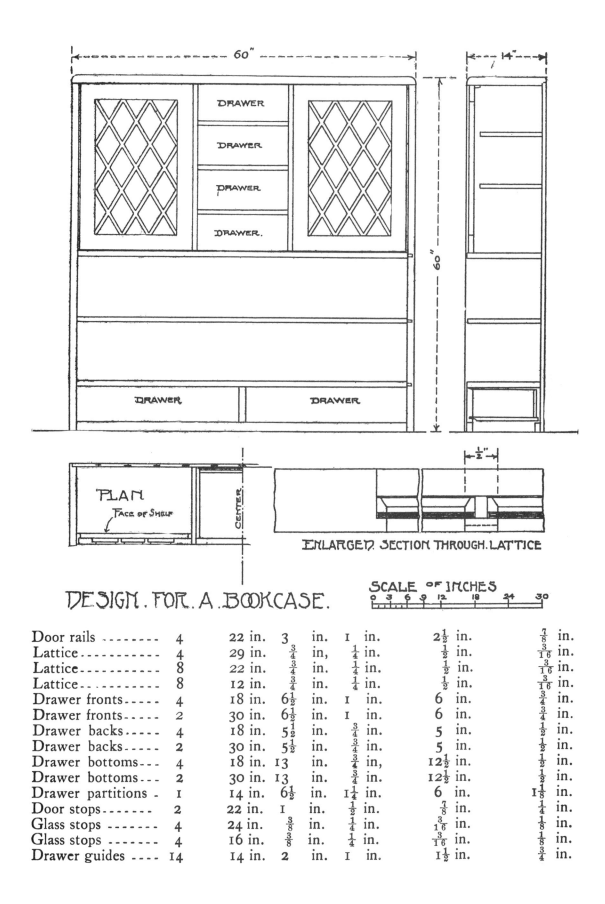

DESIGN. FOR. A. BOOKCASE.

SCALE OF INCHES
0   3   6   9   12   18   24   30

Door rails	4	22 in.	3 in.	1 in.	$2\frac{1}{2}$ in.	$\frac{7}{8}$ in.
Lattice	4	29 in.	$\frac{3}{4}$ in,	$\frac{1}{4}$ in.	$\frac{1}{2}$ in.	$\frac{3}{16}$ in.
Lattice	8	22 in.	$\frac{3}{4}$ in.	$\frac{1}{4}$ in.	$\frac{1}{2}$ in.	$\frac{3}{16}$ in.
Lattice	8	12 in.	$\frac{3}{4}$ in.	$\frac{1}{4}$ in.	$\frac{1}{2}$ in.	$\frac{3}{16}$ in.
Drawer fronts	4	18 in.	$6\frac{1}{2}$ in.	1 in.	6 in.	$\frac{3}{4}$ in.
Drawer fronts	2	30 in.	$6\frac{1}{2}$ in.	1 in.	6 in.	$\frac{3}{4}$ in.
Drawer backs	4	18 in.	$5\frac{1}{2}$ in.	$\frac{3}{4}$ in.	5 in.	$\frac{1}{2}$ in.
Drawer backs	2	30 in.	$5\frac{1}{2}$ in.	$\frac{3}{4}$ in.	5 in.	$\frac{1}{2}$ in.
Drawer bottoms	4	18 in.	13 in.	$\frac{3}{4}$ in,	$12\frac{1}{2}$ in.	$\frac{1}{2}$ in.
Drawer bottoms	2	30 in.	13 in.	$\frac{3}{4}$ in.	$12\frac{1}{2}$ in.	$\frac{1}{2}$ in.
Drawer partitions	1	14 in.	$6\frac{1}{2}$ in.	$1\frac{1}{4}$ in.	6 in.	$1\frac{1}{8}$ in.
Door stops	2	22 in.	1 in.	$\frac{1}{2}$ in.	$\frac{7}{8}$ in.	$\frac{1}{4}$ in.
Glass stops	4	24 in.	$\frac{3}{8}$ in.	$\frac{1}{4}$ in.	$\frac{3}{16}$ in.	$\frac{1}{8}$ in.
Glass stops	4	16 in.	$\frac{3}{8}$ in.	$\frac{1}{4}$ in.	$\frac{3}{16}$ in.	$\frac{1}{8}$ in.
Drawer guides	14	14 in.	2 in.	1 in.	$1\frac{1}{2}$ in.	$\frac{3}{4}$ in.

A BEDSTEAD.

The construction of the bedstead will be found one of the easiest given in our series of cabinet work but should be one of the most satisfactory. Care must be taken in making the keys which hold the side rails so that the end wood will not break out when the key is driven into place. The strips on the side rails are to be screwed in place, using six or eight screws on each rail.

MILL BILL FOR BEDSTEAD

Piecec	No.	Long	ROUGH Wide	Thick	FINISH Wide	Thick
Posts	2	62 in.	$4\frac{1}{2}$ in.	$1\frac{1}{2}$ in.	4 in.	$1\frac{3}{8}$ in.
Posts	2	53 in.	$4\frac{1}{4}$ in.	$1\frac{1}{2}$ in.	4 in.	$1\frac{3}{8}$ in.
Side rails	2	87 in.	$9\frac{1}{2}$ in.	$1\frac{1}{2}$ in.	9 in.	$1\frac{1}{4}$ in.
Side rail strips	2	77 in.	$2\frac{1}{2}$ in.	$1\frac{1}{4}$ in.	3 in.	1 in.
Top rails	4	42 in.	3 in.	$1\frac{1}{4}$ in.	$2\frac{1}{2}$ in.	1 in.
Lower rails	2	42 in.	$5\frac{1}{2}$ in.	$1\frac{1}{4}$ in.	5 in.	1 in.
Foot ballusters	6	32 in.	$3\frac{1}{2}$ in.	$\frac{3}{4}$ in.	3 in.	$\frac{5}{8}$ in.
Head ballusters	6	42 in.	$3\frac{1}{2}$ in.	$\frac{3}{4}$ in.	3 in.	$\frac{5}{8}$ in.

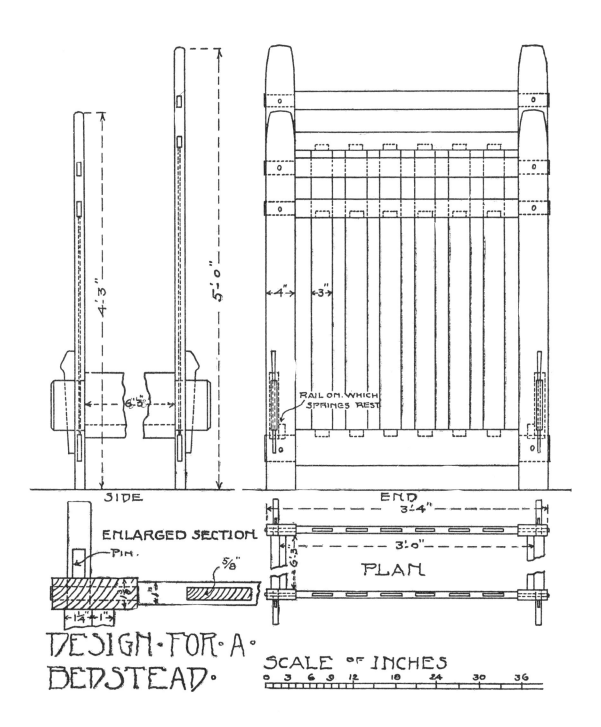

SIDE

END

ENLARGED SECTION

PIN.

RAIL ON WHICH SPRINGS REST

PLAN

DESIGN·FOR·A· BEDSTEAD·

SCALE °F INCHES

CHILD'S HIGH CHAIR

THE construction of this chair is very similar to the desk chair on pages 14–15 of this edition. The back slats are curved in the same way and the seat rails are tenoned and dowelled in a like manner. The arms of the adjustable tray are cut from a single piece of wood, and the back ends are splined by sawing straight in, to a point beyond the curve and inserting in the opening made by the saw, a piece of wood cut with the grain and well glued so giving strength to a point that would otherwise be very weak. Pages 14–15 also show the method of upholstering the seat.

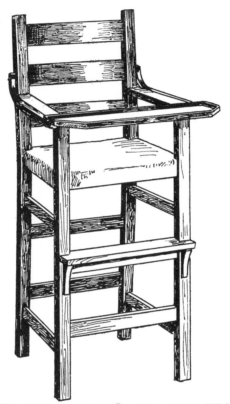

MILL BILL FOR CHILD'S HIGH CHAIR.

Pieces	No.	Long	Rough Wide	Thick	Finish Wide	Thick
Front posts	2	30 in.	1½ in.	1½ in.	1¼ in.	1¼ in.
Back posts	2	39 in.	3 in.	1½ in.	pattern	1¼ in.
Arms	2	16 in.	2½ in.	1 in.	pattern	¾ in.
Seat rails	4	14 in.	1¾ in.	1 in.	1½ in.	¾ in.
Back slats	3	14 in.	2½ in.	½ in.	2¼ in.	⅜ in.
Step	1	15 in.	3½ in.	1 in.	3 in.	¾ in.
Side stretchers	4	15 in.	1½ in.	¾ in.	1½ in.	½ in.
F. and B. stretchers.	4	15 in.	1½ in.	¾ in.	1¼ in.	½ in.
Brackets	2	5 in.	2½ in.	1 in.	pattern	¾ in.
Tray	1	20 in.	6½ in.	½ in.	6 in.	⅜ in.
Tray strips	4	20 in.	½ in.	⅜ in.	⅜ in.	¼ in.
Tray Arms	2	16 in.	4 in.	¾ in.	pattern	⅝ in.

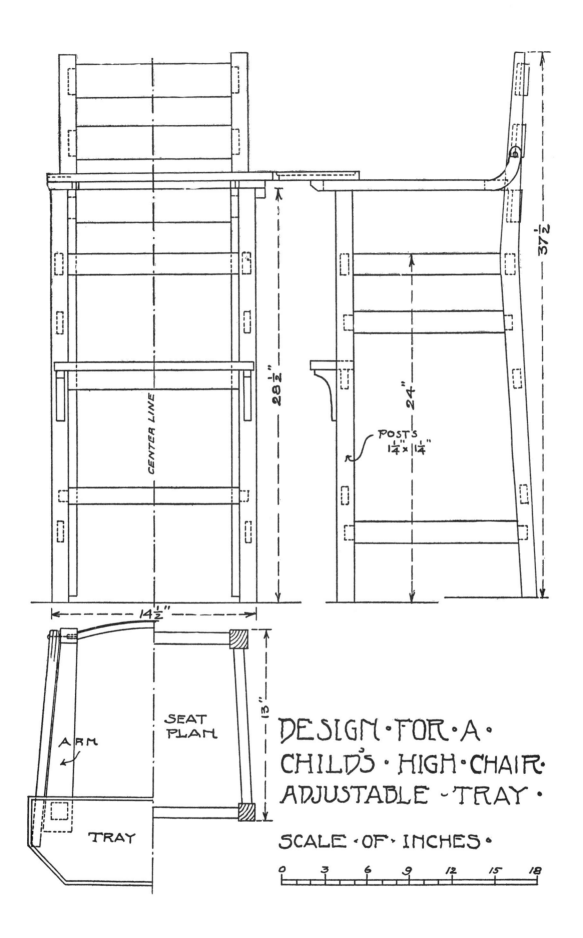

CENTER LINE

$37\frac{1}{2}$

$28\frac{1}{2}$"

24"

POSTS
$1\frac{1}{4}$" x $1\frac{1}{4}$"

$14\frac{1}{2}$"

13"

ARM

SEAT
PLAN

TRAY

DESIGN · FOR · A ·
CHILD'S · HIGH · CHAIR ·
ADJUSTABLE · TRAY ·

SCALE · OF · INCHES ·

0   3   6   9   12   15   18

SWING SEAT

A swing seat made on the lines of this one is a very simple piece to construct. The posts are halved into the seat rails and fastened with two dowell pins. The back and end slats are tenoned into the seat rails and the seat itself is made comfortable by weaving in a bottom of cane. This will stand the weather, and if the swing were used on an exposed porch there would be no fear of warping as in a broad wood seat. Use oak or chestnut fumed brown for the wood with wrought iron chains.

MILL BILL OF LUMBER FOR SWING SEAT

Pieces	No.	Long	ROUGH Wide	Thick	FINISH Wide	Thick
Post	1	23 in.	2½ in.	2½ in.	2⅜ in.	2⅜ in.
Back rail........	1	48 in.	4¼ in.	1⅜ in.	4 in.	1¼ in.
End rail........	2	22 in.	4¼ in.	1⅜ in.	4 in.	1¼ in.
Slats	5	15 in.	8¼ in.	¾ in.	8 in.	½ in.
Seat rails........	2	56 in.	3½ in.	2 in.	3¼ in.	1¾ in.
End rails........	2	17 in.	4¼ in.	2 in.	4 in.	1¾ in.

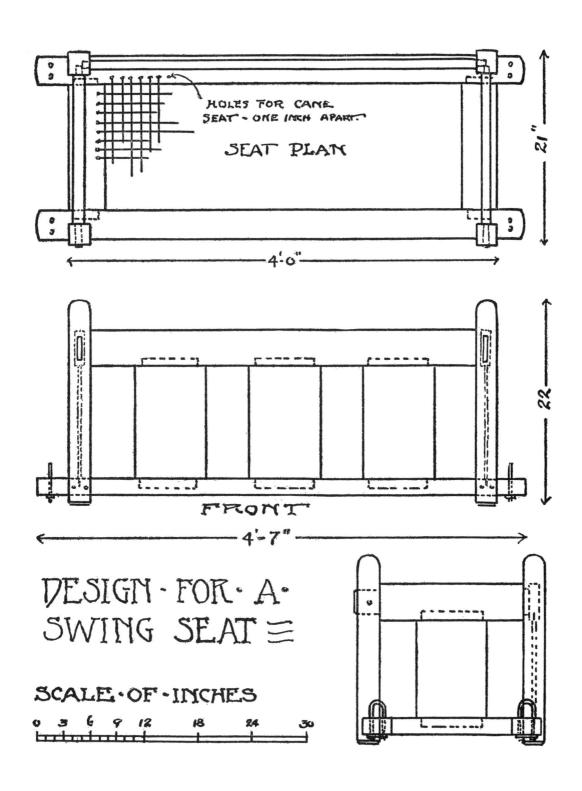

HOLES FOR CANE
SEAT - ONE INCH APART.

SEAT PLAN

21"

4'-0"

22

FRONT

4'-7"

DESIGN · FOR · A ·
SWING SEAT ≡

SCALE · OF · INCHES

0   3   6   9   12   18   24   30

WALL CABINET

THIS piece is very simple in construction, but an unusually graceful design. Its beauty is much enhanced by the work done with the gouge on the sharp curve that appears in the top line of the back, and that occurs again in the bracket under the door. As will be noted, the cutting is deep at the sharpest point of the curve, and fades away gradually as the curve flattens. The front edge of the small bracket underneath is also cut away. The edge of the shelf under the floor is rounded, and the top is shaped underneath into a very flat ogee moulding. The long strap hinges, which are good in design and clever in construction, are of hammered brass. This cabinet is very convenient as a storage place for valued trifles and also to hold a few favorite books.

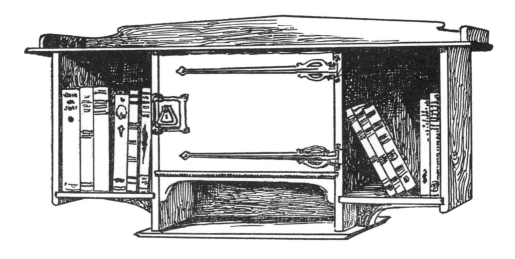

MILL BILL OF LUMBER FOR WALL CABINET.

Pieces	No.	Long	Rough Wide	Thick	Finish Wide	Thick
Top	1	35 in.	10½ in.	¾ in.	10 in.	½ in.
Top of Back	1	35 in.	3½ in.	½ in.	3 in.	⅜ in.
Top of end	2	9 in.	1½ in.	½ in.	1¼ in.	⅜ in.
Sides	2	11 in.	8¾ in.	¾ in.	8½ in.	½ in.
Partition	2	13 in.	8¾ in.	¾ in.	8½ in.	½ in.
Door	1	14 in.	8½ in.	½ in.	8¼ in.	⅜ in.
Cleat on door	2	8 in.	1¾ in.	½ in.	1½ in.	⅜ in.
Bottom of cupboard	1	15 in.	9 in.	½ in.	8½ in.	⅜ in.
Bottom of sides	2	9 in.	9 in.	½ in.	8½ in.	⅜ in.
Bottom of shelf	1	17 in.	9½ in.	½ in.	9 in.	⅜ in.
Back	1	13 in.	31 in.	½ in.	30 in.	⅜ in.
Cupboard bracket	1	15 in.	2½ in.	½ in.	pattern	⅜ in.
Under bracket	1	8 in.	3 in.	½ in.	pattern	⅜ in.

DESIGN · FOR · A · WALL · CABINET ·

SCALE · OF · INCHES ·

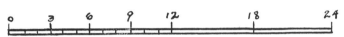

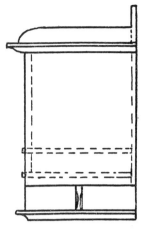

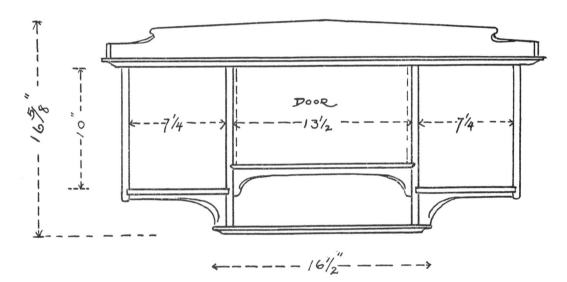

DOOR
13½

7¼   7¼

16⅝"

10"

16½"

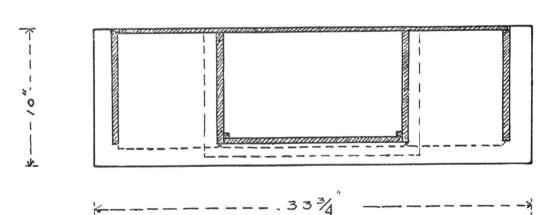

10"

33¾"

HANGING BOOK SHELF

THIS is a very useful piece of house furniture that is simple and easy to build. The working drawing shows exactly the method of construction. The best method of fastening the piece together is to screw the shelves to the back, and to fasten the back itself with small round-headed screws. The convenience of this piece will be apparent at a glance. It may either be used as a book shelf, or to hold many other things, such as bottles and small toilet accessories in a sleeping room or bath room.

MILL BILL OF LUMBER FOR HANGING BOOK SHELF

Pieces	No.	Long	Rough Wide	Thick	Finish Wide	Thick
Back posts.......	2	27 in.	3¼ in.	1 in.	3 in.	¾ in.
Top of back......	1	33 in.	6 in.	¾ in.	pattern	½ in.
Center of back....	1	14 in.	32 in.	¾ in.	31 in.	½ in.
Lower rail back...	1	33 in.	6 in.	¾ in.	pattern	½ in.
Shelves	2	36 in.	6 in.	¾ in.	5¾ in.	⅝ in.
End slats........	4	14 in.	1¾ in.	½ in.	1½ in.	⅜ in.
Brackets	2	6 in.	5 in.	1 in.	pattern	⅞ in.

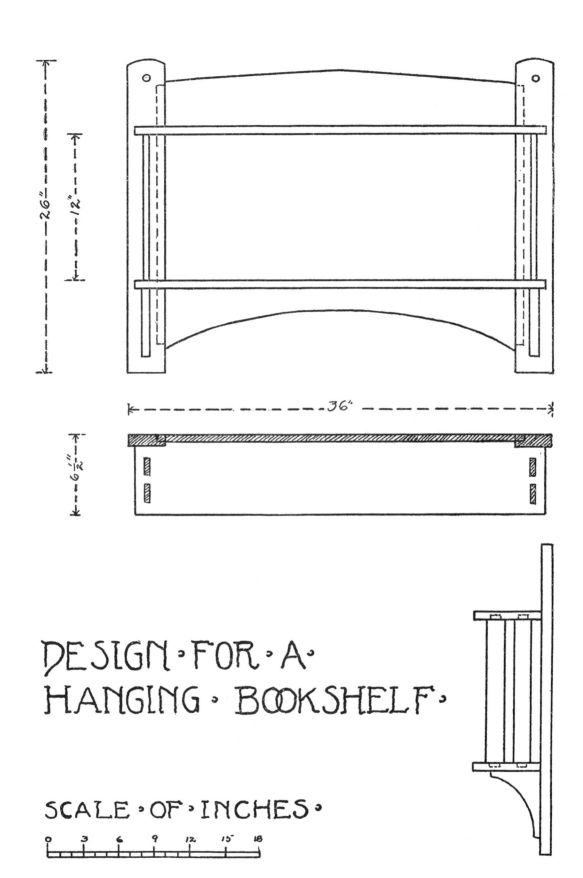

DESIGN·FOR·A·
HANGING·BOOKSHELF·

SCALE·OF·INCHES·

0   3   6   9   12   15   18

45

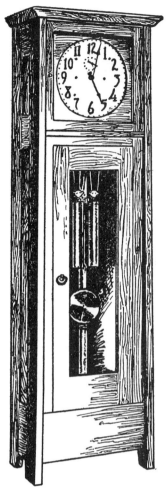

A HALL CLOCK

THERE is no more appropriate and decorative piece of furniture for a hall or large stair landing than a tall clock of the type usually known as a "grandfather's clock." Given a moderate skill in the handling of tools, and the home worker can easily make a clock that will prove a quaint and satisfactory bit of furnshing, and will furthermore give all the charm of an individual bit of handicraft made for the place it is to fill.

Oak is the most appropriate wood for the case of the hall clock. The face is made of a twelve-inch plate of brass with figures of copper. Holes are drilled in the plate which receive pins riveted on the figures. These pins are simply bent over after the figures are in place.

An inch and three-quarter 18 gauge brass tube is used for a tubular chime. This should be five feet long and suspended so that the striking hammer hits it near the point of suspension. The door at the back has a silk panel in it so that the sound easily passes through. The wood square against which the face fits can be stained a soft grey-green, if the outside is in brown fumed oak, making a charming change of color.

MILL BILL OF LUMBER FOR HALL CLOCK

Pieces	No.	Long	Rough Wide	Thick	Finish Wide	Thick
Top	1	22 in.	14½ in.	1½ in.	14 in.	1⅜ in.
Side stiles	4	72 in.	4¼ in.	1½ in.	4 in.	1⅜ in.
Side rails	4	6 in.	4¼ in.	1½ in.	4 in.	1⅜ in.
Side rails	2	6 in.	6¼ in.	1½ in.	6 in.	1⅜ in.
Side panels	2	10 in.	6¼ in.	¾ in.	6 in.	½ in.
Side panels	2	48 in.	6¼ in.	¾ in.	6 in.	½ in.
Square door	4	15 in.	1¼ in.	1¼ in.	1 in.	1 in.
Square door stop..	2	15 in.	1 in.	1½ in.	pattern	1¼ in.
Face circle	1	15 in.	15 in.	½ in.	pattern	⅜ in.
Shelf	1	16 in.	12¼ in.	1 in.	12 in.	¾ in.
Long door stiles...	2	48 in.	3 in.	1 in.	2¾ in.	¾ in.
Long door rail....	1	9 in.	4¼ in.	1 in.	4 in.	¾ in.
Long door rail....	1	9 in.	6¼ in.	1 in.	6 in.	¾ in.
Long door stops...	2	50 in.	3½ in.	1¼ in.	pattern	1⅛ in.

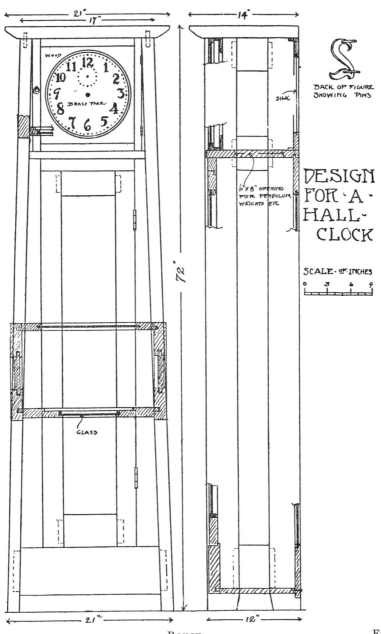

DESIGN FOR·A· HALL· CLOCK

SCALE·2·INCHES

Pieces	No.	Long	Rough Wide	Thick	Finish Wide	Thick
Long door stop...	1	14 in.	2¼ in.	1¼ in.	2 in.	1⅛ in.
Base rail	1	20 in.	6¼ in.	1½ in.	6 in.	1¼ in.
Back door	4	15 in.	2¾ in.	1 in.	2½ in.	¾ in.
Back door stops...	4	15 in.	1 in.	1 in.	¾ in.	⅞ in.
Back panel	1	46 in.	14¼ in.	¾ in.	14 in.	½ in.
Back panel stiles..	2	46 in.	4¼ in.	1 in.	4 in.	⅞ in.
Back panel rails...	2	21 in.	7¼ in.	1 in.	7 in.	⅞ in.
Bottom	1	20 in.	10¼ in.	¾ in.	10 in.	½ in.

MANTEL AND WALL CLOCKS

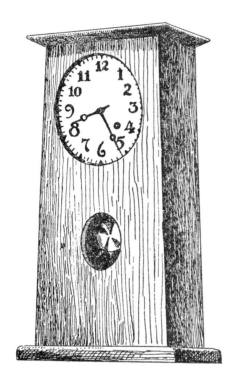

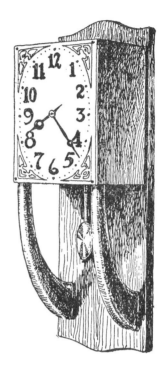

A CLOCK more than almost any other piece, needs to show fine workmanship, must be made from well seasoned wood, have perfect joints and be well finished. In these clocks attention is called to the following points: The faces are made of boxwood and the figures burned in. All the corners are well rounded by sanding. In the wall clock the top and bottom are doweled on and the back screwed in place with four screws. All are made to fit Seth Thomas clock movements.

MILL BILL OF LUMBER FOR MANTEL CLOCK

Pieces	No.	Long	Rough Wide	Thick	Finish Wide	Thick
Base	1	13 in.	5½ in.	1 in.	5¼ in.	¾ in.
Top	1	12 in.	6 in.	1 in.	5¾ in.	¾ in.
Sides	2	18 in.	5 in.	1 in.	4¾ in.	¾ in.
Front	1	18 in.	10 in.	½ in.	pattern	⅜ in.
Back	1	18 in.	10 in.	¾ in.	pattern	½ in.
Face	1	8 in.	8 in.	3-16 in.	7½ in.	⅛ in.

MILL BILL OF LUMBER FOR WALL CLOCK

Pieces	No.	Long	Rough Wide	Thick	Finish Wide	Thick
Back	1	16 in.	7 in.	¾ in.	6½ in.	⅝ in.
Sides	4	7 in.	4 in.	¾ in.	3½ in.	½ in.
Brackets	2	8 in.	3 in.	1 in.	pattern	pattern
Face	1	7 in.	7 in.	3-16 in.	6 in.	⅛ in.

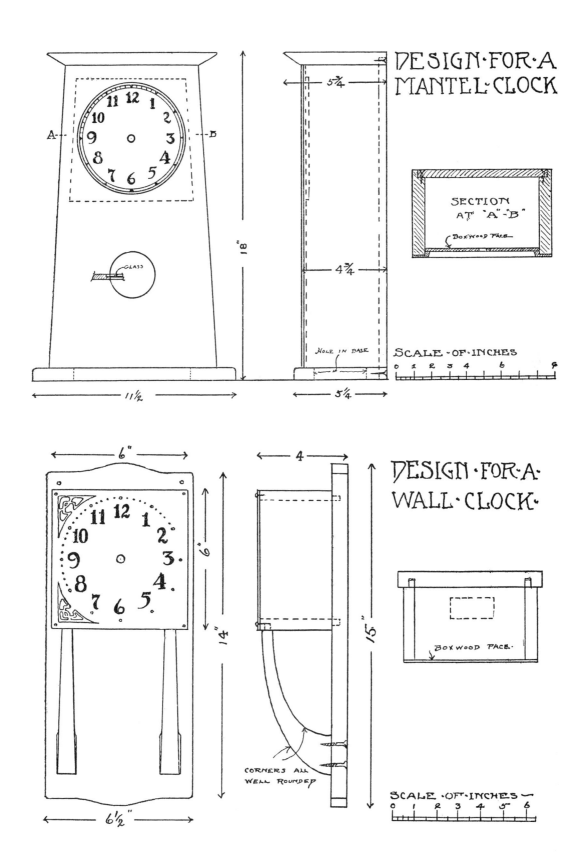

DESIGN·FOR·A
MANTEL·CLOCK

A —— B

18"

11½"

5¾

4¾

GLASS

HOLE IN BASE

5¼

SECTION
AT "A"-"B"

BOXWOOD FACE

SCALE·OF·INCHES
0 1 2 3 4 6 5

DESIGN·FOR·A
WALL·CLOCK·

6"

4

6"

14"

15"

6½"

BOXWOOD FACE.

CORNERS ALL
WELL ROUNDED

SCALE·OF·INCHES
0 1 2 3 4 5 6

49

A WRITING TABLE

THIS design, which is given in response to a request from a subscriber interested in cabinet work, will be found very satisfactory for a writing table. The construction is not at all hard, the main point being to have the lower parts firmly fastened to the top with table irons, and the brace at the center firmly fastened at the ends. This is necessary that the drawer may run smoothly. The feature of special note in this table is the recessed book shelf at either end, which solves the problem of having reference books within easy reach of the writer.

MILL BILL OF LUMBER FOR WRITING TABLE

Pieces	No.	Long	Rough Wide	Thick	Finish Wide	Thick
Legs	4	29 in.	2 in.	2 in.	1¾ in.	1¾ in.
Top	1	45 in.	28¼ in.	1¼ in.	28 in.	1 in.
Front stiles	8	12 in.	3¾ in.	1 in.	3½ in.	⅞ in.
Front rails	8	6 in.	3¼ in.	1 in.	3 in.	⅞ in.
Front panels	4	6 in.	5¼ in.	¾ in.	5 in.	½ in.
Back center rail..	1	24 in.	4¼ in.	1 in.	4 in.	⅞ in.
Back of book rack.	2	25 in.	10¼ in.	1 in.	10 in.	⅞ in.
Under brace	1	24 in.	4¼ in.	1¼ in.	4 in.	1⅛ in.
Drawer front	1	24 in.	4¼ in.	1 in.	4 in.	⅞ in.
Drawer sides, back	3	24 in.	4¼ in.	¾ in.	4 in.	½ in.
Drawer bottom...	1	24 in.	22 in.	¾ in.	21½ in.	½ in.
Drawer runners ..	2	24 in.	¾ in.	¾ in.	½ in.	½ in.

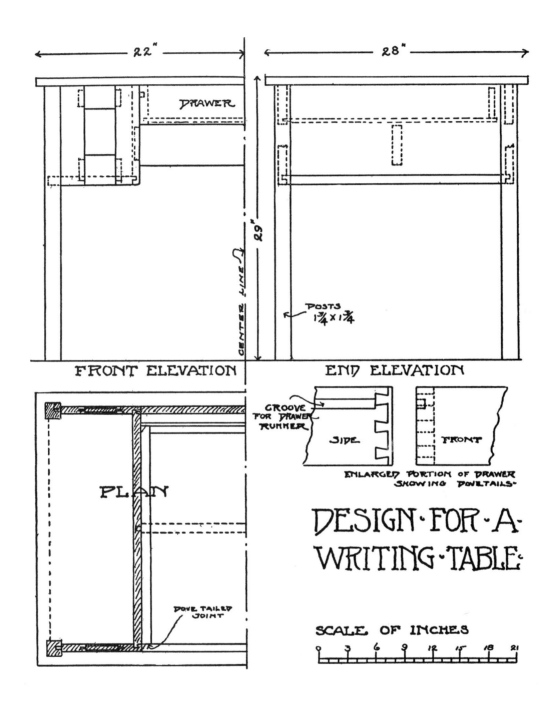

22"

DRAWER

28"

29"

CENTER LINE

POSTS
1¾ x 1¾

FRONT ELEVATION

END ELEVATION

GROOVE
FOR DRAWER
RUNNER

SIDE

FRONT

ENLARGED PORTION OF DRAWER
SHOWING DOVETAILS·

PLAN

DOVE TAILED
JOINT

DESIGN · FOR · A ·
WRITING · TABLE·

SCALE OF INCHES

0   3   6   9   12   15   18   21

A MORRIS CHAIR

THIS model is given in response to a number of requests for a Morris chair that could be made at home. The construction is very simple. The sides are put together first, then the front and back seat rails. The seat frame is pierced with holes placed about an inch apart, and through these is to be woven cane or heavy cord to afford a firm and elastic support for the seat cushion. Either one is satisfactory, but the cane will be found more durable. The seat pillow should be from four to five inches thick; the back pillow from five to six inches thick and high enough to cover the top slat in the back.

MILL BILL OF LUMBER FOR MORRIS CHAIR

Pieces	No.	Long	Rough Wide	Thick	Finish Wide	Thick
Posts	4	21 in.	2½ in.	2½ in.	2¼ in.	2¼ in.
Arms	2	37 in.	4¾ in.	1¼ in.	4½ in.	1⅛ in.
Front rail	1	27 in.	5¼ in.	1½ in.	5 in.	1¼ in.
Back rail........	1	27 in.	3¼ in.	1½ in.	3 in.	1¼ in.
Side rail........	2	27 in.	5¼ in.	1½ in.	5 in.	1¼ in.

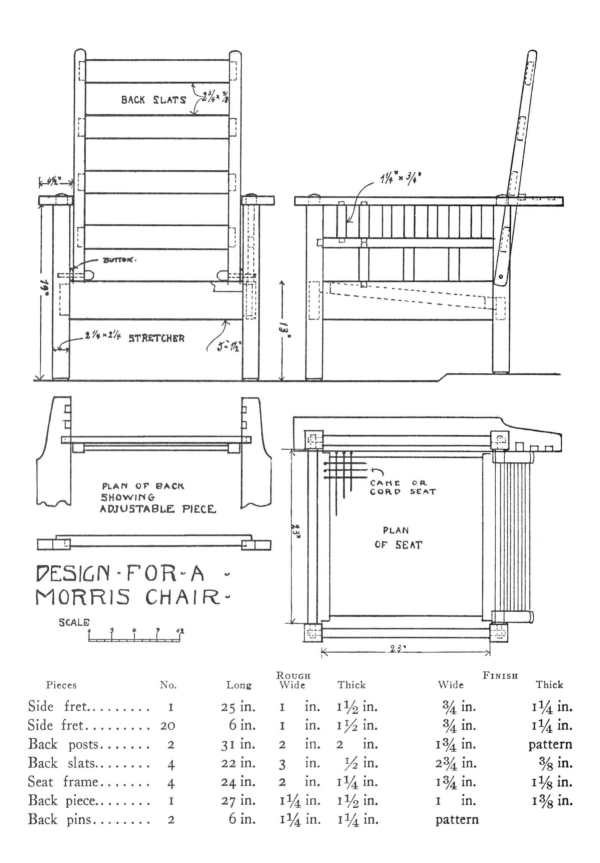

BACK SLATS 2¾ × ⅜

4½"

19"

BUTTON.

2¼ × 2¼ STRETCHER

5 × 1½"

1¼" × ¾"

13"

PLAN OF BACK
SHOWING
ADJUSTABLE PIECE

CANE OR
CORD SEAT

PLAN
OF SEAT

23"

23"

DESIGN·FOR·A·
MORRIS CHAIR·

SCALE

Pieces	No.	Long	Rough Wide	Rough Thick	Finish Wide	Finish Thick
Side fret.........	1	25 in.	1 in.	1½ in.	¾ in.	1¼ in.
Side fret.........	20	6 in.	1 in.	1½ in.	¾ in.	1¼ in.
Back posts.......	2	31 in.	2 in.	2 in.	1¾ in.	pattern
Back slats........	4	22 in.	3 in.	½ in.	2¾ in.	⅜ in.
Seat frame.......	4	24 in.	2 in.	1¼ in.	1¾ in.	1⅛ in.
Back piece........	1	27 in.	1¼ in.	1½ in.	1 in.	1⅜ in.
Back pins........	2	6 in.	1¼ in.	1¼ in.	pattern	

53

DINING TABLE

THIS table is designed to extend to ten feet. The extension slides will need to be procured from a manufacturer as they are difficult to make by hand. The center leg is firmly screwed on to the cross piece and each end of the cross piece is screwed to the center slide of each group. Four dowel pins keep the top exactly flush and ordinary window fasteners, if placed at the joining of the rails, will keep them from parting. Blocks are glued and screwed to the rails and lag screws run through these blocks and the leg, making a very firm joint, which is necessary on account of there being no support below. The top is fastened by table irons about 9 inches apart, one being placed in the top of each leg and the others spaced evenly on the rails.

MILL BILL OF LUMBER FOR DINING TABLE

Pieces	No.	Long	Rough Wide	Thick	Finish Wide	Thick
Legs	5	30 in.	4¼ in.	4¼ in.	4 in.	4 in.
Top	2	55 in.	28 in.	1½ in.	pattern	1⅜ in.
Rails	4	30 in.	7 in.	5¼ in.	pattern	5 in.
Center brace	1	30 in.	5¼ in.	1½ in.	5 in.	1¼ in.
Leaves	5	55 in.	13½ in.	1½ in.	13 in.	1⅜ in.
Blocks for rails	8	6 in.	4 in.	2½ in.	pattern	pattern

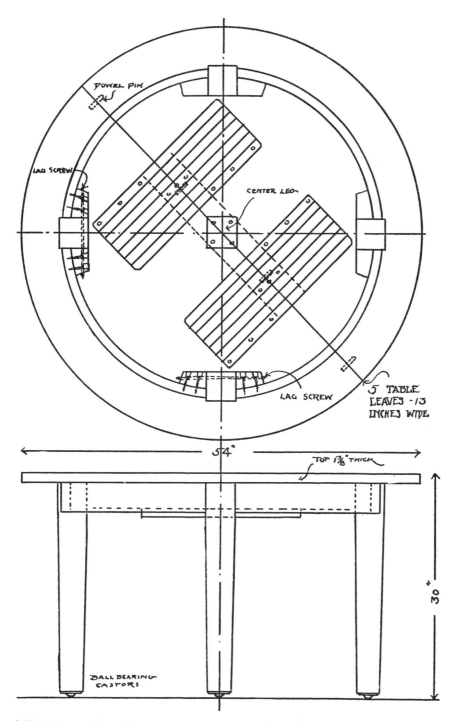

DOWEL PIN

LAG SCREW

CENTER LEG

LAG SCREW

5 TABLE
LEAVES - 13
INCHES WIDE

54"

TOP 1⅞" THICK

30"

BALL BEARING
CASTORS

DESIGN·FOR·AN·EXTENSION·
DINING·TABLE

SCALE OF INCHES
0 3 6   12   21

55

SIDE CHAIR

IN general the same directions apply to the side chair as to the arm chair.* The seats of both may be made comfortable by first stretching webbing over the frame, then muslin and a very thin layer of curled hair and covering with a good quality of soft leather. The chairs made of oak and fumed to a dark rich brown might have leather of moss green and dull brass nails.

MILL BILL OF LUMBER FOR SIDE DINING CHAIR

Pieces	No.	Long	Rough Wide	Thick	Finish Wide	Thick
Front posts......	2	19 in.	1½ in.	1½ in.	1⅝ in.	1⅝ in.
Back posts.......	2	40 in.	3½ in.	1⅝ in.	pattern	1½ in.
Seat rails........	4	16 in.	2¾ in.	1 in.	2½ in.	⅞ in.
Side stretchers....	4	15 in.	2 in.	¾ in.	1¾ in.	⅝ in.
F. &. B. stretchers.	2	17 in.	2¼ in.	¾ in.	2 in.	⅝ in.
Top back slat.....	1	16 in.	2¼ in.	1 in.	2 in.	¾ in.
Lower back slat...	1	16 in.	2 in.	1 in.	1¾ in.	¾ in.
Upright slats.....	2	15 in.	1½ in.	¾ in.	1¼ in.	⅝ in.
Strips on side rails.	2	15 in.	1 in.	1 in.	⅞ in.	⅞ in.

*See pages 4, 30 and especially 14 in this edition.

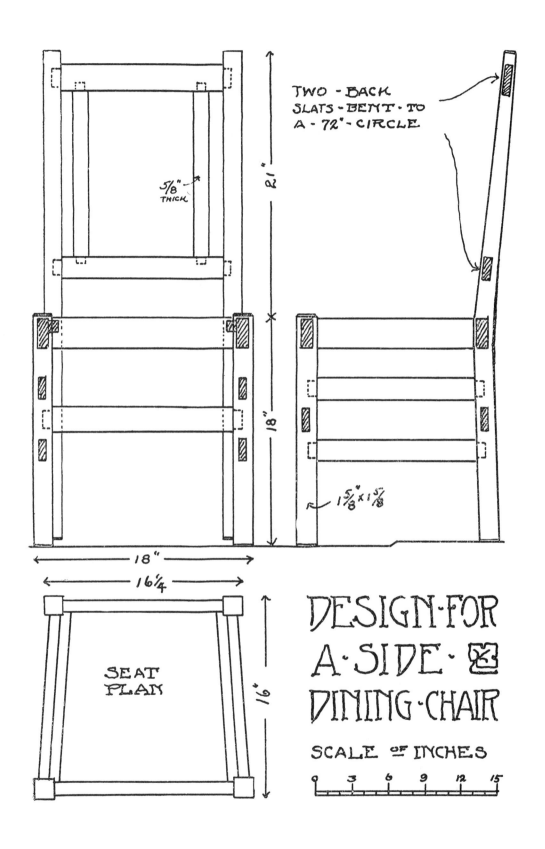

5/8" THICK

21"

TWO · BACK
SLATS · BENT · TO
A · 72° · CIRCLE

18"

1 5/8" x 1 5/8"

18"

16 1/4"

16"

SEAT
PLAN

DESIGN · FOR
A · SIDE · 🔲
DINING · CHAIR

SCALE ᴼᶠ INCHES

0   3   6   9   12   15

A SIDEBOARD

THE lines and proportions of this small sideboard make it an unusually graceful piece. The back is to be screwed into place and is put on last. The top can be dowelled on or, if there is any doubt as to the thorough seasoning of the wood, fastened with table irons. The irons will admit of a slight shrinkage or swell without cracking the wood. All the edges should be slightly softened with sandpaper just before the finish is applied.

MILL BILL OF LUMBER FOR SIDEBOARD

Pieces	No.	Long	Rough Wide	Thick	Finish Wide	Thick
Top	1	55 in.	20½ in.	1¼ in.	20 in.	1⅛ in.
Legs	4	39 in.	2½ in.	2½ in.	2¼ in.	2¼ in.
Top of back	1	55 in.	4 in.	1⅛ in.	pattern	1 in.
Shelves	2	49 in.	20 in.	1 in.	19½ in.	¾ in.
Drawer fronts	4	17 in.	4¼ in.	1 in.	4 in.	⅞ in.
Drawer sides	8	18 in.	4¼ in.	⅝ in.	4 in.	½ in.
Drawer backs	4	17 in.	4¼ in.	¾ in.	4 in.	½ in.
Drawer bottoms	4	17 in.	18½ in.	½ in.	18 in.	⅜ in.
Drawer front	1	46 in.	6¼ in.	1 in.	6 in.	⅞ in.
Drawer sides	2	18 in.	6¼ in.	¾ in.	6 in.	½ in.

DESIGN·FOR·SIDEBOARD

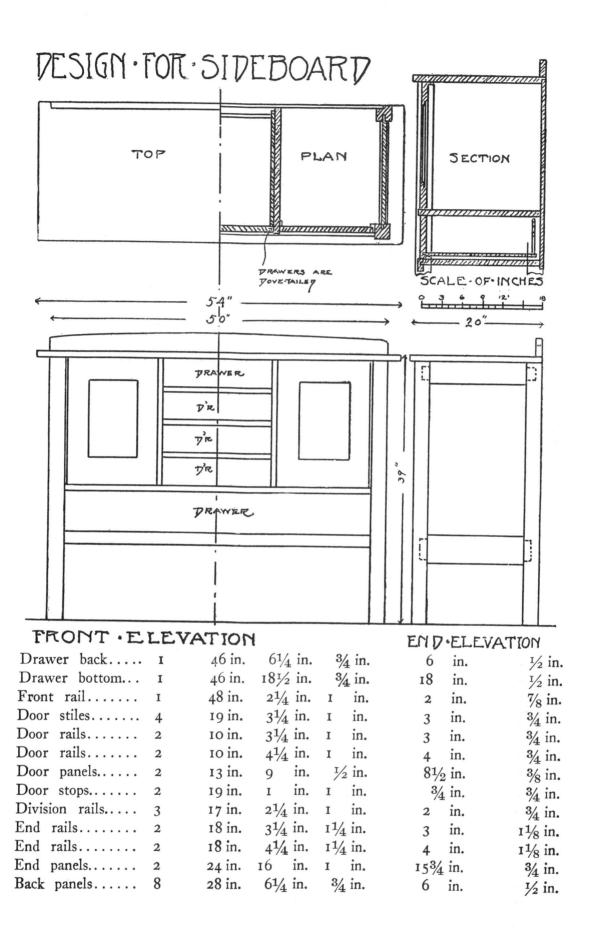

TOP

PLAN

SECTION

DRAWERS ARE
DOVE·TAILED

SCALE·OF·INCHES

0 3 6 9 12 18

54"

50"

20"

DRAWER

D'R

D'R

D'R

DRAWER

39"

FRONT·ELEVATION

END·ELEVATION

Drawer back.....	1	46 in.	6¼ in.	¾ in.	6 in.	½ in.
Drawer bottom...	1	46 in.	18½ in.	¾ in.	18 in.	½ in.
Front rail......	1	48 in.	2¼ in.	1 in.	2 in.	⅞ in.
Door stiles.......	4	19 in.	3¼ in.	1 in.	3 in.	¾ in.
Door rails.......	2	10 in.	3¼ in.	1 in.	3 in.	¾ in.
Door rails.......	2	10 in.	4¼ in.	1 in.	4 in.	¾ in.
Door panels......	2	13 in.	9 in.	½ in.	8½ in.	⅜ in.
Door stops.......	2	19 in.	1 in.	1 in.	¾ in.	¾ in.
Division rails.....	3	17 in.	2¼ in.	1 in.	2 in.	¾ in.
End rails........	2	18 in.	3¼ in.	1¼ in.	3 in.	1⅛ in.
End rails........	2	18 in.	4¼ in.	1¼ in.	4 in.	1⅛ in.
End panels.......	2	24 in.	16 in.	1 in.	15¾ in.	¾ in.
Back panels......	8	28 in.	6¼ in.	¾ in.	6 in.	½ in.

SETTLE

AS in the arm chair,*the arms of the settle are put on after the rest of the piece is put together. The back rails are perfectly straight and no filling is needed under the leather in the back. Upholster the seat as described for the side and arm chairs.† To make this piece strong after the stretchers are put in, three-eighth inch pins may be put through the leg, fastening the tenon. The back rails may also be pinned in the same way. Note also the quarter inch pin which is put into the back of the arm after the arm is in place.

MILL BILL OF LUMBER FOR A HIGH BACK SETTLE

Pieces	No.	Long	Rough Wide	Thick	Finish Wide	Thick
Front posts......	2	25 in.	2½ in.	2½ in.	2¼ in.	2¼ in.
Back posts.......	2	54 in.	3½ in.	2½ in.	pattern	2¼ in.
Arms	2	26 in.	5 in.	1½ in.	pattern	pattern
Seat rails........	2	50 in.	5¼ in.	1¼ in.	5 in.	1⅛ in.
Seat rails........	2	22 in.	5¼ in.	1¼ in.	5 in.	1⅛ in.
Stretchers	2	51 in.	2¼ in.	1 in.	2 in.	¾ in.
Stretchers	2	22 in.	1¾ in.	1 in.	1½ in.	¾ in.
Back rail.........	1	51 in.	3 in.	1 in.	2¾ in.	¾ in.
Back rail........	1	51 in.	2¼ in.	1 in.	2 in.	¾ in.
Back rails........	2	31 in.	2¼ in.	1 in.	2 in.	¾ in.

*Arm chair is on page 30.

†Side chair is on page 56.

4' 0"

4' 4½"

19"

23½"

PIN

DESIGN · FOR · A · HIGH · BACK · SETTLE

SCALE OF INCHES
0   3   6   9   15   21

A PLATE RACK

THE plate rack given here is so simple in construction that nothing need be said excepting that the brackets are fastened with screws from the back. This piece would serve as a stein rack for a den as well as a plate rack for the dining-room and be quite as appropriate. It is designed to hang from the picture rail by chains from either side; plain round link chains can be purchased ready-made or can be made to order by any blacksmith, together with the hooks.

MILL BILL OF LUMBER FOR PLATE RACK

Pieces	No.	Long	Rough Wide	Thick	Finish Wide	Thick
Back posts.......	2	25 in.	2¾ in.	1 in.	2½ in.	⅞ in.
Top rail........	1	45 in.	4 in.	1 in.	pattern	¾ in.
Shelf	1	46 in.	3 in.	¾ in.	2¾ in.	⅝ in.
Shelf	1	48 in.	3¾ in.	1 in.	3½ in.	¾ in.
Brackets	2	10 in.	2½ in.	1 in.	pattern	⅞ in.
Brackets	2	4 in.	3 in.	1¼ in.	pattern	1⅛ in.
Back	1	45 in.	22 in.	¾ in.	21½ in.	⅝ in.

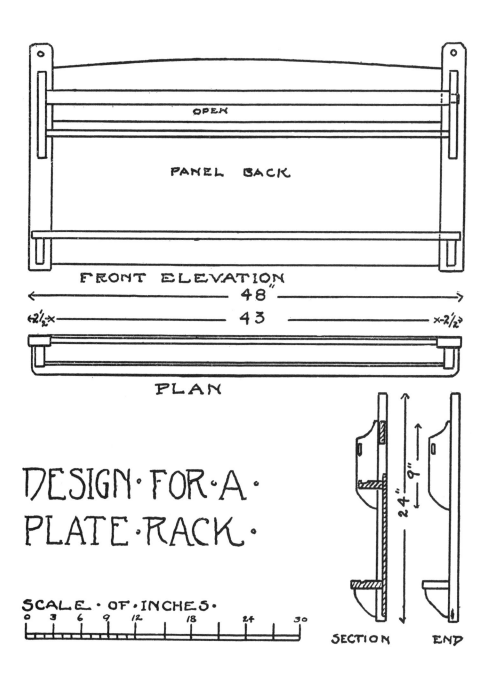

OPEN

PANEL BACK

FRONT ELEVATION

48"

←2½→ 43 ←2½→

PLAN

DESIGN·FOR·A
PLATE·RACK·

24" 9"

SECTION   END

SCALE·OF·INCHES·

0 3 6 9 12 18 24 30

CORNER CHINA CABINET

THIS piece is the most difficult of any yet given in our Cabinet Work Series. The fitting of the 45° angles must be carefully done, as these are dowelled joints. The glass mullions are halved together and demand careful work. Mortise and tenon joints must be used in putting the back together.

MILL BILL OF LUMBER FOR CORNER CABINET

Pieces	No.	Long	Rough Wide	Thick	Finish Wide	Thick
Top	1	43 in.	22 in.	1¼ in.	▽	1⅛ in.
Shelves	2	38 in.	20 in.	1 in.	▽	⅞ in.
Back stiles.......	4	60 in.	4¼ in.	1¼ in.	4 in.	1⅛ in.
Back rails........	2	22 in.	4¼ in.	1¼ in.	4 in.	1⅛ in.
Back rails........	2	22 in.	6¼ in.	1¼ in.	6 in.	1⅛ in.
Back rails........	2	22 in.	9¼ in.	1¼ in.	9 in.	1⅛ in.
Back stiles.......	4	22 in.	3¼ in.	1¼ in.	3 in.	1⅛ in.
Back panels.......	8	22 in.	9¼ in.	¾ in.	9 in.	½ in.
Inside shelves.....	3	35 in.	10¾ in.	⅞ in.	10½ in.	¾ in.

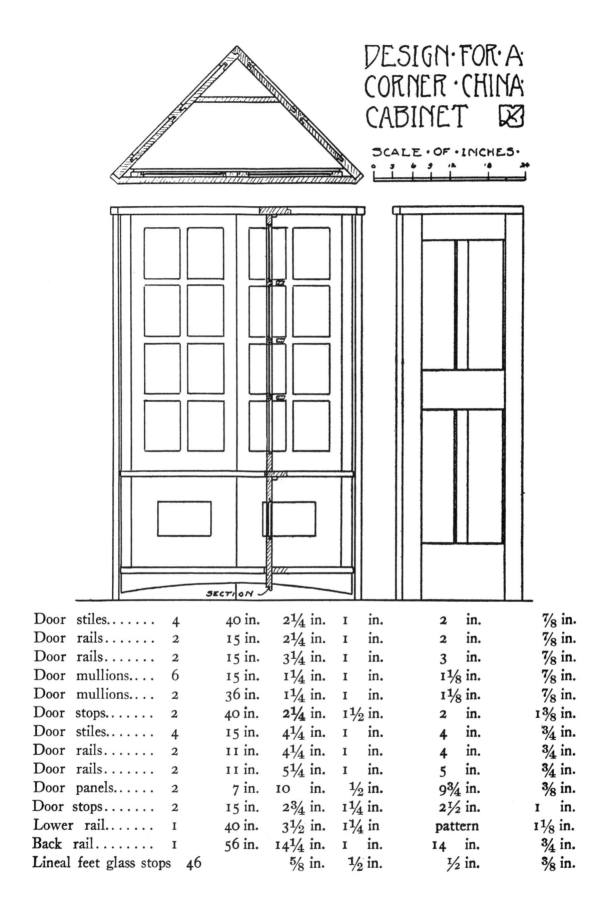

DESIGN·FOR·A·
CORNER·CHINA·
CABINET

SCALE·OF·INCHES·

SECTION

Door stiles......	4	40 in.	2¼ in.	1 in.	2 in.	⅞ in.
Door rails.......	2	15 in.	2¼ in.	1 in.	2 in.	⅞ in.
Door rails.......	2	15 in.	3¼ in.	1 in.	3 in.	⅞ in.
Door mullions....	6	15 in.	1¼ in.	1 in.	1⅛ in.	⅞ in.
Door mullions....	2	36 in.	1¼ in.	1 in.	1⅛ in.	⅞ in.
Door stops.......	2	40 in.	2¼ in.	1½ in.	2 in.	1⅜ in.
Door stiles.......	4	15 in.	4¼ in.	1 in.	4 in.	¾ in.
Door rails.......	2	11 in.	4¼ in.	1 in.	4 in.	¾ in.
Door rails.......	2	11 in.	5¼ in.	1 in.	5 in.	¾ in.
Door panels......	2	7 in.	10 in.	½ in.	9¾ in.	⅜ in.
Door stops.......	2	15 in.	2¾ in.	1¼ in.	2½ in.	1 in.
Lower rail......	1	40 in.	3½ in.	1¼ in	pattern	1⅛ in.
Back rail.......	1	56 in.	14¼ in.	1 in.	14 in.	¾ in.
Lineal feet glass stops	46		⅝ in.	½ in.	½ in.	⅜ in.

SERVING TABLE

FOR a large dining-room in addition to the sideboard a serving table seems to be a necessity, while for a small dining-room the sideboard may be dispensed with and the serving table made to answer for every purpose. The piece here given is a forty-two inch serving table and is large enough to serve for the only cabinet piece in a small room. The construction is very similar to that of the sideboard* and needs no further explanation.

MILL BILL OF LUMBER FOR SERVING TABLE

Pieces	No.	Long	Rough Wide	Thick	Finish Wide	Thick
Top	1	43 in.	16½ in.	1¼ in.	16 in.	1 in.
Legs	4	36 in.	2 in.	2 in.	1¾ in.	1¾ in.
Top of back	1	40 in.	2¾ in.	1 in.	2½ in.	⅞ in.
Shelf	1	39 in.	12½ in.	1 in.	12 in.	⅞ in.
End stretchers	2	14 in.	3¾ in.	1¼ in.	3½ in.	1⅛ in.
End panel	2	14 in.	9¼ in.	1 in.	9 in.	⅞ in.
Front rail	1	38 in.	2½ in.	1 in.	2¼ in.	⅞ in.
Drawer fronts ...	2	18 in.	3¾ in.	1 in.	3½ in.	⅞ in.
Drawer sides	4	15 in.	3¾ in.	¾ in.	3½ in.	½ in.
Drawer backs	2	18 in.	3¾ in.	¾ in.	3½ in.	½ in.

*Sideboard is on page 58.

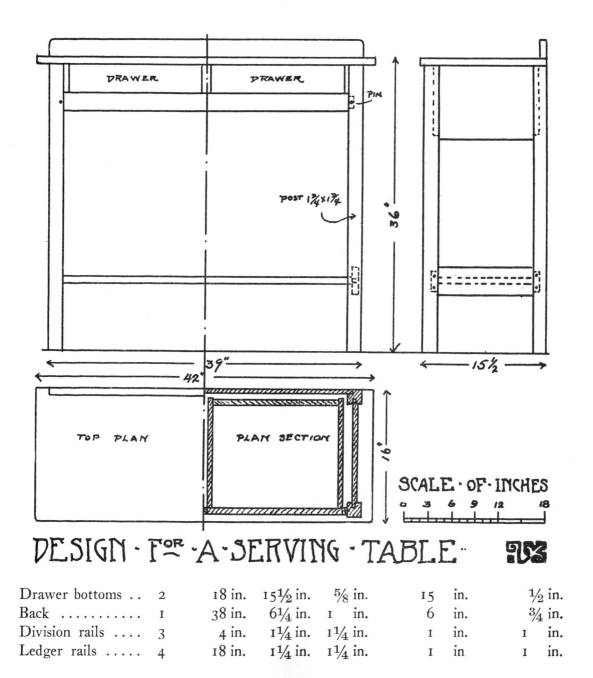

DRAWER   DRAWER

PIN

POST 1¾×1¾

36"

15½

39"

42"

TOP PLAN   PLAN SECTION

16"

SCALE · OF · INCHES
0   3   6   9   12   18

DESIGN · FOR · A · SERVING · TABLE ·

Drawer bottoms ..	2	18 in.	15½ in.	⅝ in.	15 in.	½ in.
Back	1	38 in.	6¼ in.	1 in.	6 in.	¾ in.
Division rails	3	4 in.	1¼ in.	1¼ in.	1 in.	1 in.
Ledger rails	4	18 in.	1¼ in.	1¼ in.	1 in.	1 in.

CHILD'S TABLE

THE construction of the child's table shown here is so simple as to be elementary. The top is fastened with the regular table irons, which give opportunity for any slight swell or shrinkage of the wood without checking the top. The stretcher is tenoned through the ends and is securely fastened by pegs. This little table is designed to be used with the small settle illustrated on another page of this number.*

MILL BILL OF LUMBER FOR CHILD'S TABLE

Pieces	No.	Long	Rough Wide	Thick	Finish Wide	Thick
Top	1	37 in.	24½ in.	1 in.	24 in.	¾ in.
Ends	2	22 in.	20 in.	1⅛ in.	pattern	1 in.
Braces	2	27 in.	3¼ in.	1 in.	3 in.	⅞ in.
Stretcher	1	32 in.	4¼ in.	1 in.	4 in.	⅞ in.
Pegs	2	4 in.	2 in.	1 in.	pattern	¾ in.

*Page 70 of this edition.

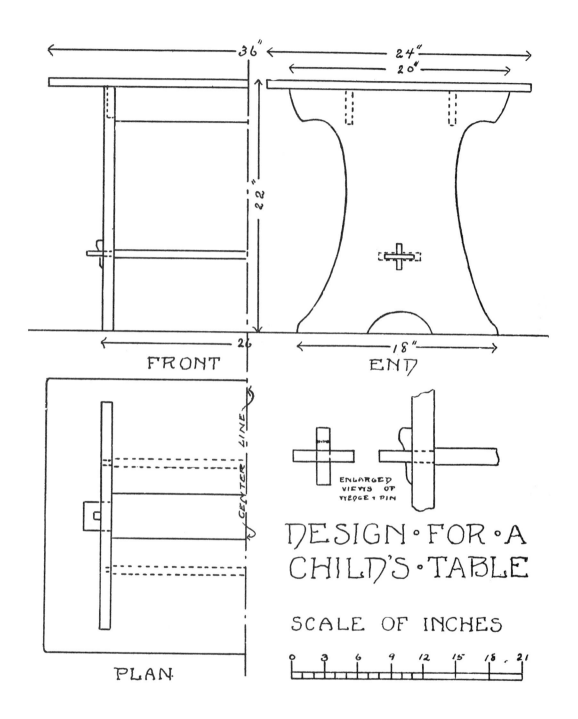

36"

24"

20"

22"

26

18"

FRONT

END

CENTER LINE

PLAN.

ENLARGED
VIEWS OF
WEDGE & PIN

DESIGN · FOR · A
CHILD'S · TABLE

SCALE OF INCHES

0   3   6   9   12   15   18   21

CHILD'S SETTLE

THIS little piece is both attractive and easily made. It is designed to be used with the child's table given in this number,* and it is well to make two settles as companion pieces to one table. The seat, braces and center back slat are tenoned and glued, and are further secured in place by the top slat and the lower brace. The tenon of the top slat extends through the end and is pinned from the back, while the tenon of the lower brace extends through and is keyed. This device adds to the beauty of the piece as well as to the firmness of its construction.

MILL BILL OF LUMBER FOR CHILD'S SETTLE

Pieces	No.	Long	Rough Wide	Thick	Finish Wide	Thick
Two ends........	1	50 in.	17 in.	1⅛ in.	pattern	1 in.
Top of back......	1	40 in.	2¼ in.	1 in.	2 in.	⅞ in.
Seat	1	40 in.	13 in.	1 in.	12½ in.	⅞ in.
Seat braces	2	40 in.	2¾ in.	1 in.	2½ in.	⅞ in.
Lower brace	1	44 in.	3¾ in.	1⅛ in.	3½ in.	1 in.
Pegs	2	4 in.	2 in.	1 in.	pattern	¾ in.
Center back slat..	1	40 in.	6¼ in.	1 in.	6 in.	⅞ in.

*Page 68 of this edition.

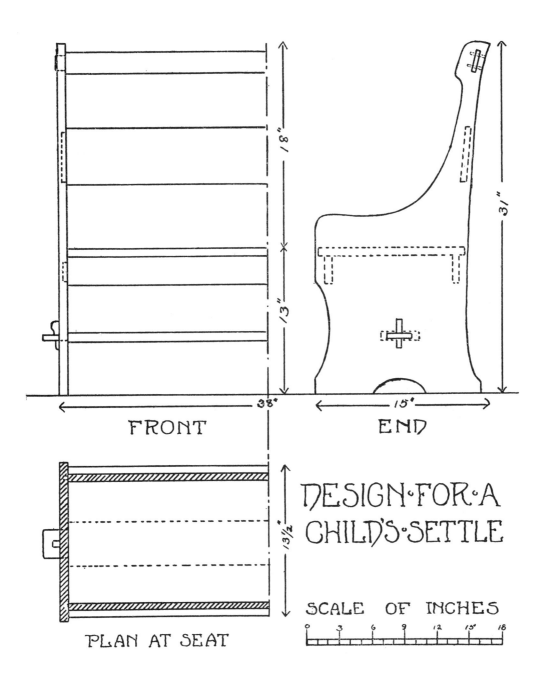

FRONT

18"

13"

38"

END

31"

15"

13½"

PLAN AT SEAT

DESIGN·FOR·A
CHILD'S·SETTLE

SCALE OF INCHES

0   3   6   9   12   15   18

BEDROOM STAND

THIS is a small table primarily designed for use in a bedroom, to stand near the bed and hold a lamp, candle or one or two books, but it is convenient in any place where a small stand is needed. The top of the back is to be dowelled in place with three half-inch dowels. The top is fastened by table fasteners placed under the wide overhang at the sides. The drawers are to be dovetailed together and all edges slightly softened by sandpapering.

MILL BILL OF LUMBER FOR BEDROOM STAND

Pieces	No.	Long	ROUGH Wide	Thick	FINISH Wide	Thick
Legs	4	29 in.	1½ in.	1½ in.	1⅜ in.	1⅜ in.
Top	1	21 in.	18 in.	1 in.	17½ in.	⅞ in.
Top of Back	1	18 in.	1¾ in.	1 in.	1½ in.	⅞ in.
Sides	2	17 in.	8¼ in.	1 in.	8 in.	¾ in.
Back	1	16 in.	8¼ in.	1 in.	8 in.	¾ in.

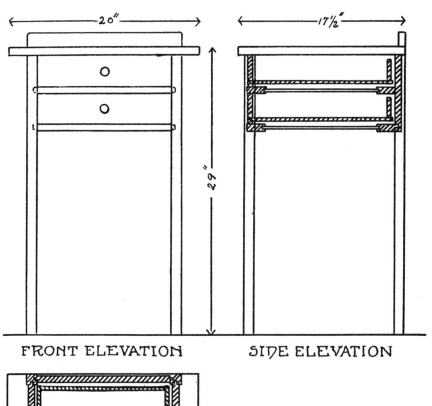

FRONT ELEVATION   SIDE ELEVATION

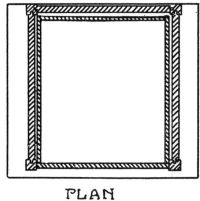

PLAN

DESIGN·FOR
A·BEDROOM
STAND ℰℰℰ

SCALE OF INCHES
0   3   6   9   12   15   18

Dust panel rails...	8	16 in.	2¼ in.	1 in.	2 in.	¾ in.
Dust panels	2	14 in.	13½ in.	⅝ in.	13 in.	½ in.
Drawer fronts ...	2	15 in.	3¼ in.	1 in.	3 in.	¾ in.
" backs ...	2	15 in.	3¼ in.	¾ in.	3 in.	½ in.
" sides	4	16 in.	3¼ in.	¾ in.	3 in.	½ in.
" bottoms..	2	14 in.	15½ in.	½ in.	15 in.	⅜ in.

HALL TABLE WITH MIRROR

A PIECE suited to any hall. Especially so on account of the width, which is three feet. Hooks of iron are best, but those of copper or brass may be used. Attention is called to the construction of the mirror frame; the rails are rabbeted five-eighths of an inch, the mirror plate is laid in place, then a triangular piece of soft pine, indicated on the drawing in solid black, is pressed firmly against the edge of the glass and fastened with small beads. The back is held in place by screws. A small drawer might be made under the table top, if desired, providing a place for the clothes brush, or a large deep drawer could be used for overshoes.

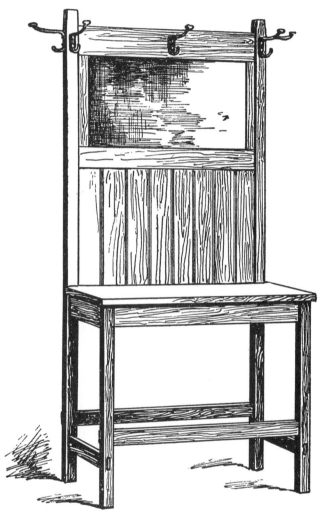

MILL BILL OF LUMBER FOR HALL TABLE WITH MIRROR

Pieces	No.	Long	Rough Wide	Thick	Finish Wide	Thick
Back posts	2	73 in.	2 in.	2 in.	1¾ in.	1¾ in.
Front posts....	2	30 in.	2 in.	2 in.	1¾ in.	1¾ in.
Stretchers	2	37 in.	2¼ in.	2¼ in.	2 in.	2 in.

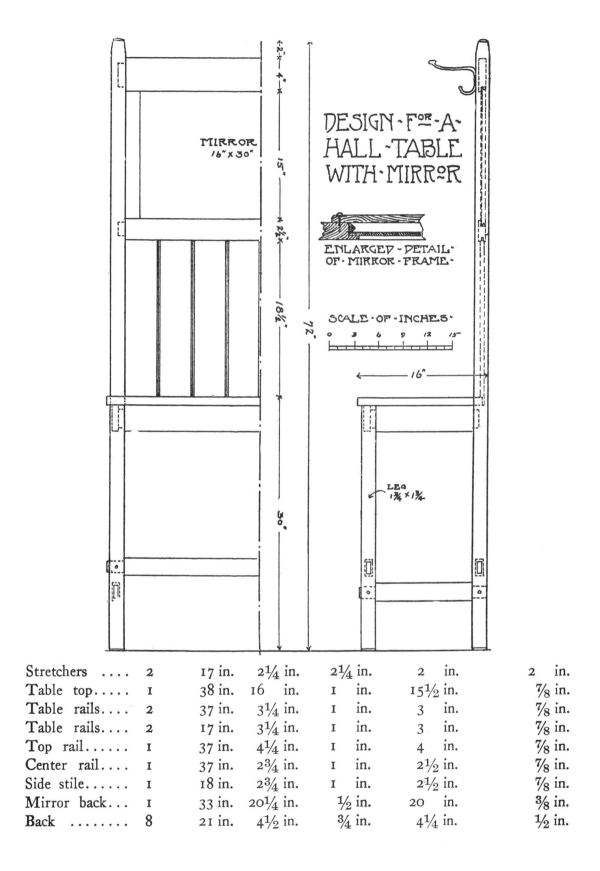

DESIGN·F⁰ᴿ·A·
HALL·TABLE
WITH·MIRROR

ENLARGED·DETAIL·
OF·MIRROR·FRAME·

SCALE·OF·INCHES·

MIRROR
16"x30"

LEG
1¾ x 1¾

16"

Stretchers	2	17 in.	2¼ in.	2¼ in.	2 in.	2 in.
Table top	1	38 in.	16 in.	1 in.	15½ in.	⅞ in.
Table rails	2	37 in.	3¼ in.	1 in.	3 in.	⅞ in.
Table rails	2	17 in.	3¼ in.	1 in.	3 in.	⅞ in.
Top rail	1	37 in.	4¼ in.	1 in.	4 in.	⅞ in.
Center rail	1	37 in.	2¾ in.	1 in.	2½ in.	⅞ in.
Side stile	1	18 in.	2¾ in.	1 in.	2½ in.	⅞ in.
Mirror back	1	33 in.	20¼ in.	½ in.	20 in.	⅜ in.
Back	8	21 in.	4½ in.	¾ in.	4¼ in.	½ in.

CHILD'S OPEN BOOKCASE

ONE of the great difficulties in attaining a tidy nursery is often that there is no place where children can easily put things away themselves. Closet-doors are hard to open and the shelves too high to be of use. Wall shelves and brackets are usually purposely out of reach, and the nursery table is apt to be full.

This child's open bookcase is planned especially to meet this nursery problem; there are no doors and the shelves are broad and low enough to be within the reach of very little children. The shelves are not adjustable but put in stoutly with tenon and key so that they are never out of place and never need attention. All furniture in a child's room should be well finished to avoid the slightest chance of slivers or scratches. It is a nice idea to finish the bookcase in harmony with the other woodwork of the nursery, unless this is in a bright tone; in which case a beautiful soft, harmonious wood tone would be best. This piece of furniture could also be used in a library or sewing-room.

MILL BILL OF STOCK FOR OPEN BOOKCASE

Pieces	No.	Rough Long	Wide	Thick	Finish Wide	Thick
Sides	2	40 in.	10½ in.	1⅛ in.	10 in.	1 in.
Top	1	20 in.	11 in.	1 in.	10½ in.	⅞ in.
Back	1	36 in.	16 in.	¾ in.	15½ in.	½ in.
Shelves	3	16½ in.	10 in.	1 in.	16 in.	⅞ in.
Stretchers	2	18½ in.	3 in.	1¼ in.	pattern	1⅛ in.

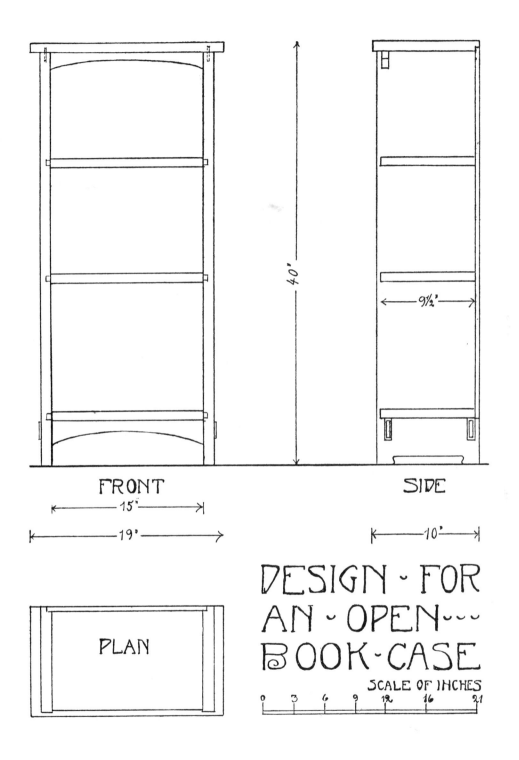

FRONT

15"

19"

40"

SIDE

9½"

10"

PLAN

DESIGN · FOR
AN · OPEN ···
BOOK · CASE

SCALE OF INCHES

0   3   6   9   12   16   21

SPINDLE-BED FOR CHILD

FROM the time a child graduates from a crib, this design of a small Craftsman bed is appropriate. It is made after the new spindle pattern which is so popular in other models of Craftsman furniture. Although having the effect of a grown-up bed, it is, nevertheless, enough smaller than the standard adult size to delight a child for years. This bed is planned to be made in the most substantial fashion, and is put together in the same durable way as the finest piece of grown-up furniture. It is made low so that a child can easily get in and out without help. As with all other children's furniture, the home cabinet-maker is advised to finish as carefully as possible to avoid any injury to little nursery folk. The most complete detail for the making of this piece of furniture is given in the working plan on the opposite side of the page.

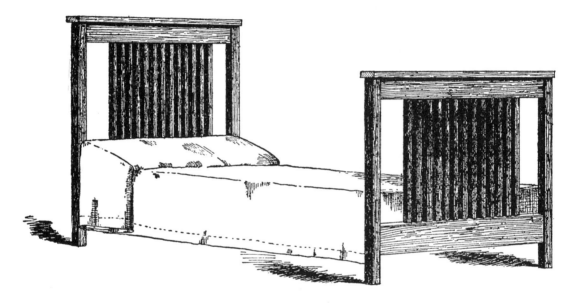

MILL BILL OF STOCK FOR CHILD'S BED

Pieces	No.	Rough Long	Wide	Thick	Finish Wide	Thick
Posts	2	44 in.	2¼ in.	2¼ in.	2 in.	2 in.
Posts	2	34 in.	2¼ in.	2¼ in.	2 in.	2 in.
Top	2	38 in.	3½ in.	1¼ in.	3 in.	1 in.
Top rails	2	36 in.	4 in.	1¼ in.	3½ in.	1⅛ in.
Lower rails	2	36 in.	5½ in.	1¼ in.	5 in.	1⅛ in.
Spindles	13	32 in.	1⅛ in.	1⅛ in.	1 in.	1 in.
Spindles	13	22 in.	1⅛ in.	1⅛ in.	1 in.	1 in.
Side rails	2	5 x 11 in.	6½ in.	1¼ in.	6 in.	1⅛ in.

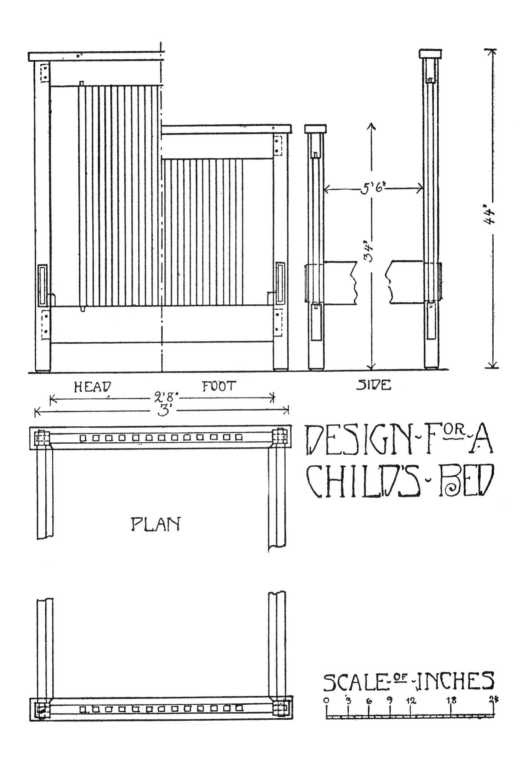

HEAD   FOOT   SIDE

5'6"

34"

44"

2'8"

3'

PLAN

DESIGN·FOR·A
CHILD'S·BED

SCALE·OF·INCHES

0   3   6   9   12   18   24

CHILD'S DRESSER

THERE are no gifts which children appreciate so much and so long as furnishings for their own room, and a complete room can be fitted up without much expense if every birthday and Christmas brings an article of furniture. And if this furniture can be made by some member of the family, a child's delight is doubled.

The Craftsman bureau shown on this page is intended to be made with the utmost care, so that finished, it would be beautiful and durable and a life-long possession. In the plans shown on the opposite page you will see that every detail is carefully worked out. The drawers are all made with dust panels underneath, and it is intended that the inside finish of them should be fine and velvety. By careful study of the working-plan, such a dresser could be put together by any amateur cabinet-maker.

MILL BILL OF STOCK FOR CHILD'S DRESSER

Pieces	No.	Rough Long	Wide	Thick	Finish Wide	Thick
Posts	4	30 in.	2¼ in.	2¼ in.	2 in.	2 in.
Top	1	43 in.	20½ in.	1⅛ in.	20 in.	1 in.
Sides	2	26 in.	18 in.	1 in.	17¾ in.	⅞ in.
Drawer fronts	2	18 in.	4½ in.	1 in.	4 in.	⅞ in.
Drawer sides	4	18½ in.	4½ in.	¾ in.	4 in.	½ in.
Drawer backs	2	18 in.	4½ in.	¾ in.	3¾ in.	½ in.
Drawer bottoms	2	17½ in.	17½ in.	⅝ in.	17¼ in.	½ in.
Drawer front	1	37 in.	7½ in.	1 in.	7¼ in.	⅞ in.
Drawer sides	2	18½ in.	7½ in.	¾ in.	7¼ in.	½ in.
Drawer backs	1	37 in.	7½ in.	¾ in.	7 in.	½ in.
Drawer bottoms	1	36½ in.	17½ in.	⅝ in.	17¼ in.	½ in.
Drawer front	1	37 in.	9½ in.	1 in.	9 in.	⅞ in.

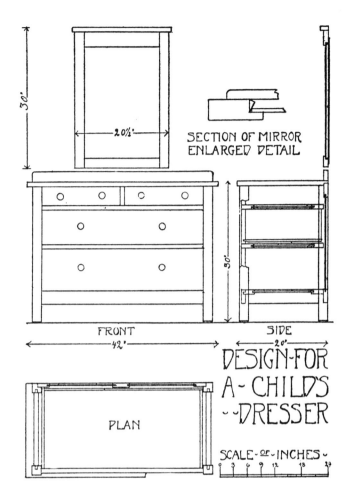

SECTION OF MIRROR
ENLARGED DETAIL

FRONT

SIDE

PLAN

DESIGN·FOR
A~ CHILD'S
~·DRESSER

SCALE·℥·INCHES·

Drawer sides	2	18½ in.	9½ in.	¾ in.	9 in.	½ in.
Drawer backs	1	37 in.	9½ in.	¾ in.	8¾ in.	½ in.
Drawer bottoms	1	36½ in.	17½ in.	⅝ in.	17¼ in.	½ in.
Back rails	2	38 in.	3¾ in.	1 in.	3½ in.	¾ in.
Back stiles	3	27 in.	3¾ in.	1 in.	3½ in.	¾ in.
Back panels	2	21 in.	21 in.	½ in.	20 in.	⅜ in.
Division rails	6	38 in.	3½ in.	1 in.	3 in.	¾ in.
Ledger rails	7	19 in.	3½ in.	1 in.	3 in.	¾ in.

MILL BILL OF STOCK FOR MIRROR

Pieces	No.	Rough			Finish	
		Long	Wide	Thick	Wide	Thick
Top	1	22-in.	2 in.	1 in.	1¾ in.	⅞ in.
Top rail	1	19½ in.	3½ in.	1 in.	3¼ in.	⅞ in.
Lower rail	1	19½ in.	2¼ in.	1 in.	2 in.	⅞ in.
Stiles	2	29½ in.	2¼ in.	1 in.	2 in.	⅞ in.

A PIANO BENCH

THIS piano bench is simplicity itself in design, yet so cunningly are its proportions contrived that it is very decorative in effect. The outward slope of the solid end pieces gives an appearance of great strength that does full justice to the real strength of the piece. The severity of these end pieces is rather lightened by the curved opening at the bottom, and by the openings at the top meant for convenience in moving the bench. The only decoration is the slight projection of the tenons at the ends.

MILL BILL OF STOCK FOR BENCH.

Pieces.	No.	Rough			Finish	
		Long	Wide	Thick	Wide	Thick
Top	1	40 in.	15½ in.	1⅛ in.	15 in.	1 in.
Sides	2	25½ in.	17½ in.	1¼ in.	pattern	1⅛ in.

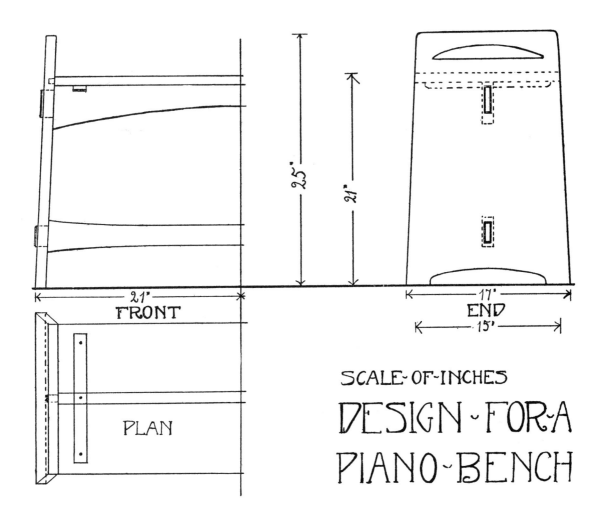

FRONT

PLAN

END

SCALE·OF·INCHES

DESIGN·FOR·A
PIANO·BENCH

Top stretcher 1	41¾ in.	4¼ in.	1½ in.	pattern	1¼ in.
Lower stretcher ... 1	42½ in.	3½ in.	1½ in.	pattern	1¼ in.
Top braces 2	14 in.	1¾ in.	¾ in.	1½ in.	⅝ in.

ROUND TABLE.

THE round table shown here has the same general features in its construction as the library table,* only modified to such a degree that the effect is light rather than massive. The braces, top and bottom, are crossed, and the four legs are wide and flat, with openings following the lines of the outside, and the decorative structural features of key and tenon made prominent. This table would be very useful in the living-room or as a second table in a large library, or it might be the main reading-table in a study or den.

MILL BILL OF STOCK FOR ROUND TABLE.

Pieces.	No.	Long	Rough. Wide	Thick	Finished. Wide	Thick
Top	1	41 in.	41 in.	1⅛ in.	40 in. diam.	1 in.
Legs	4	29 in.	5¼ in.	1¼ in.	pattern	1⅛ in.
Top stretcher	2	34 in.	3¾ in.	1⅜ in.	3½ in.	1¼ in.
Lower stretcher ...	2	37 in.	2¾ in.	1⅜ in.	2½ in.	1¼ in.
Shelf	1	19 in.	19 in.	1 in.	18 in. diam.	⅞ in.

*Page 100 of this edition.

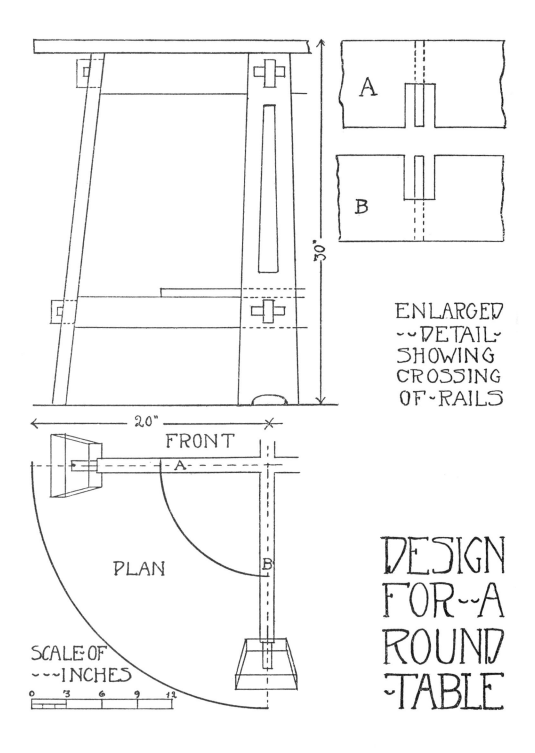

A

B

ENLARGED
~~DETAIL~
SHOWING
CROSSING
OF~RAILS

30"

20"

FRONT

A

PLAN

B

SCALE OF
~~~INCHES

0   3   6   9   12

DESIGN
FOR~A
ROUND
~TABLE

DESIGNS and working drawings for one or two articles of bedroom furniture have been asked for by some of our friends interested in home cabinet work, so we here present two pieces not included among the designs for bedroom furniture already published, but in harmony with them, so that all easily might form one set. The shaving stand shown on this page is a simply-made but substantial little affair, with the usual sturdy mortise-and-tenon construction that is decorative as well as useful. A small cupboard is provided to hold the larger shaving utensils, and a drawer where the razors may be kept free from dust and moisture. The shaving-glass is supported on a firmly braced standard, held in place by a stout wooden pin. Knobs of wood are used on drawer and cupboard door instead of metal pulls.

MILL BILL OF LUMBER FOR SHAVING STAND

Pieces	No.	Long	Rough Wide	Thick	Finish Wide	Thick
Legs	4	46 in.	1½ in.	1½ in.	1¼ in.	1¼ in.
Top	1	18 in.	16 in.	1 in.	14 in.	⅞ in.
Sides	2	16 in.	13 in.	1 in.	11½ in.	⅞ in.
Back	1	16 in.	13 in.	¾ in.	12½ in.	½ in.
Door	1	13 in.	10 in.	1 in.	9½ in.	⅞ in.
Drawer front	1	13 in.	4¼ in.	1 in.	4 in.	¾ in.
Drawer sides	2	11 in.	4 in.	⅝ in.	3¾ in.	½ in.

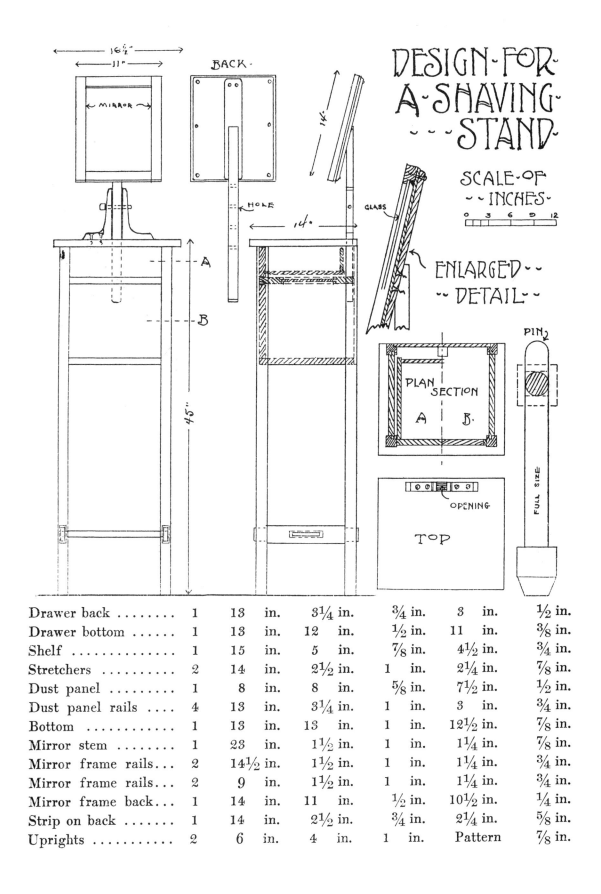

DESIGN·FOR·
A·SHAVING·
···STAND·

SCALE·OF·
··INCHES·

ENLARGED··
··DETAIL·~

Drawer back	1	13 in.	3¼ in.	¾ in.	3 in.	½ in.
Drawer bottom	1	13 in.	12 in.	½ in.	11 in.	⅜ in.
Shelf	1	15 in.	5 in.	⅞ in.	4½ in.	¾ in.
Stretchers	2	14 in.	2½ in.	1 in.	2¼ in.	⅞ in.
Dust panel	1	8 in.	8 in.	⅝ in.	7½ in.	½ in.
Dust panel rails	4	13 in.	3¼ in.	1 in.	3 in.	¾ in.
Bottom	1	13 in.	13 in.	1 in.	12½ in.	⅞ in.
Mirror stem	1	23 in.	1½ in.	1 in.	1¼ in.	⅞ in.
Mirror frame rails...	2	14½ in.	1½ in.	1 in.	1¼ in.	¾ in.
Mirror frame rails...	2	9 in.	1½ in.	1 in.	1¼ in.	¾ in.
Mirror frame back...	1	14 in.	11 in.	½ in.	10½ in.	¼ in.
Strip on back	1	14 in.	2½ in.	¾ in.	2¼ in.	⅝ in.
Uprights	2	6 in.	4 in.	1 in.	Pattern	⅞ in.

AN EASY CHAIR FOR THE VERANDA

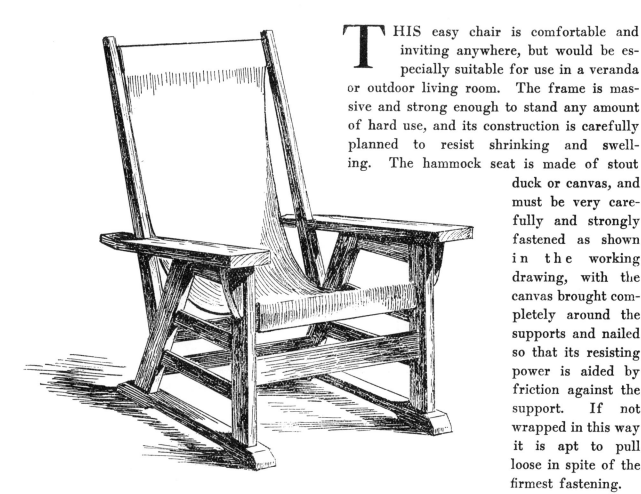

THIS easy chair is comfortable and inviting anywhere, but would be especially suitable for use in a veranda or outdoor living room. The frame is massive and strong enough to stand any amount of hard use, and its construction is carefully planned to resist shrinking and swelling. The hammock seat is made of stout duck or canvas, and must be very carefully and strongly fastened as shown in the working drawing, with the canvas brought completely around the supports and nailed so that its resisting power is aided by friction against the support. If not wrapped in this way it is apt to pull loose in spite of the firmest fastening.

MILL BILL OF LUMBER FOR EASY CHAIR

Pieces	No.	Long	Rough Wide	Thick	Finish Wide	Thick
Posts	4	21 in.	$3\frac{1}{4}$ in.	$1\frac{1}{2}$ in.	3 in.	$1\frac{1}{4}$ in.
Arms	2	36 in.	$5\frac{1}{4}$ in.	$1\frac{1}{4}$ in.	5 in.	$1\frac{1}{8}$ in.
Front rail	1	25 in.	3 in.	$1\frac{1}{2}$ in.	$2\frac{3}{4}$ in.	$1\frac{1}{4}$ in.
Front rail	1	25 in.	$3\frac{1}{2}$ in.	1 in.	$3\frac{1}{4}$ in.	$\frac{3}{4}$ in.
Side rails	4	20 in.	2 in.	$\frac{3}{4}$ in.	$1\frac{3}{4}$ in.	$\frac{5}{8}$ in.
Side rails	2	14 in.	3 in.	$\frac{3}{4}$ in.	$2\frac{3}{4}$ in.	$\frac{5}{8}$ in.
Back rails	2	25 in.	$2\frac{1}{4}$ in.	$\frac{3}{4}$ in.	2 in.	$\frac{5}{8}$ in.

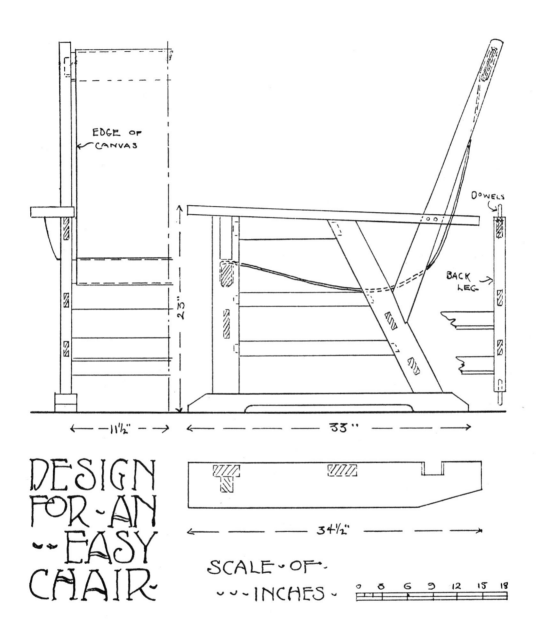

EDGE OF CANVAS

DOWELS

BACK LEG

23"

11½"

33"

34½"

DESIGN
FOR·AN
··EASY
CHAIR·

SCALE·OF·
··~·INCHES·

0   3   6   9   12   15   18

Base rails	2	35 in.	3 in.	2½ in.	2⅝ in.	2¼ in.
Brackets	2	5 in.	2 in.	1¾ in.	1¾ in.	1½ in.
Back posts	2	35 in.	3 in.	1½ in.	Pattern	1¼ in.
Back slat	1	25 in.	4 in.	1 in.	3½ in.	⅞ in.

CRAFTSMAN BOOKCASE FOR ENCYCLOPEDIA

AN ENCYCLOPEDIA is rapidly becoming an essential part of the furnishings, not only of the home library but of the sitting-room, where much reading or studying is done. The family circle who read much nowadays wants to read intelligently, and this is only to be accomplished by convenient reference books; and books to be convenient must be close at hand, placed near the table or desk, ready to use without much lifting or reaching out. The CRAFTSMAN encyclopedia bookcase is designed to meet just this condition, to furnish convenient reference to busy people without especial exertion. The model here given is an essentially simple piece of furniture with complete and easily understood working plans. The usual encyclopedia set comprises twenty volumes, but the shelves of this bookcase are so divided that there are twenty-one spaces, so that a dictionary also may always be at hand.

MILL BILL OF LUMBER FOR ENCYCLOPEDIA BOOKCASE

Pieces	No.	Long	Rough Wide	Thick	Finish Wide	Thick
Sides	2	48 in.	13 in.	1½ in.	12 in.	1¼ in.
Top	1	21 in.	14½ in.	1 in.	14 in.	⅞ in.
Cleat	1	21 in.	1¾ in.	⅞ in.	1½ in.	¾ in.
Front Rail	1	18 in.	1¾ in.	1¾ in.	1½ in.	Shaped

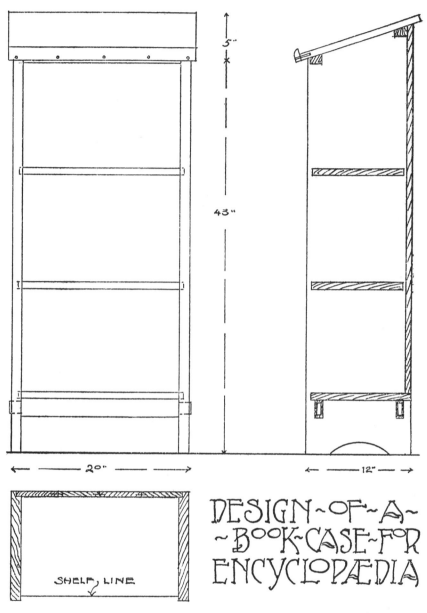

5"

43"

20"

12"

SHELF LINE

DESIGN~OF~A~
~BOOK~CASE~FOR
ENCYCLOPÆDIA

SCALE OF INCHES ~~ 0 3 6 9 12 15 18

Part	Qty					
Front Rail	1	21 in.	$2\frac{1}{4}$ in.	$1\frac{1}{4}$ in.	2 in.	1 in.
Back Rail	1	18 in.	$1\frac{3}{4}$ in.	$1\frac{3}{4}$ in.	$1\frac{1}{2}$ in.	$1\frac{1}{2}$ in.
Back Rail	1	21 in.	$2\frac{1}{4}$ in.	$1\frac{1}{4}$ in.	2 in.	1 in.
Shelves	3	19 in.	13 in.	1 in.	$12\frac{1}{2}$ in.	$\frac{7}{8}$ in.
Backs	4	42 in.	5 in.	$\frac{3}{4}$ in.	$4\frac{3}{4}$ in.	$\frac{5}{8}$ in.

THERE is no article of miniature furniture that children so delight in as a desk, where they can work like grown-up folks, and have pads and pencils never to be loaned or lost, and a real air of adult industry. Children not only enjoy a small desk, but actually work better at one. To please the young mind it is necessary to make things for work or play along simple lines. Children are essentially primitive, and resent fussy over-ornamentation which they do not understand. For this reason, it is inevitable that they should like CRAFTSMAN furniture, and, as a matter of fact, they always do. A child's CRAFTSMAN desk, which is very simple in construction, is a very worth-while desk to little members of the family—who would also even enjoy helping to make it.

MILL BILL OF LUMBER FOR CHILD'S DESK

Pieces	No.	Long	Rough Wide	Thick	Finish Wide	Thick
Legs	2	31 in.	1½ in.	1½ in.	1⅜ in.	1⅜ in.
Legs	2	24 in.	1½ in.	1½ in.	1⅜ in.	1⅜ in.
Top	1	27 in.	22 in.	⅞ in.	21½ in.	¾ in.
Top	1	25 in.	7 in.	⅝ in.	6 in.	½ in.
Front Rail	1	24 in.	1¼ in.	1 in.	1 in.	⅞ in.
Side Stretchers	2	20 in.	2¼ in.	⅞ in.	2 in.	¾ in.
Back Stretchers	1	25 in.	2¼ in.	⅞ in.	3 in.	¾ in.
Side Rails	2	19 in.	4¼ in.	1 in.	4 in.	⅞ in.
Sides	2	6 in.	5 in.	⅝ in.	4½ in.	½ in.
Partition	1	6 in.	5 in.	½ in.	4½ in.	⅜ in.

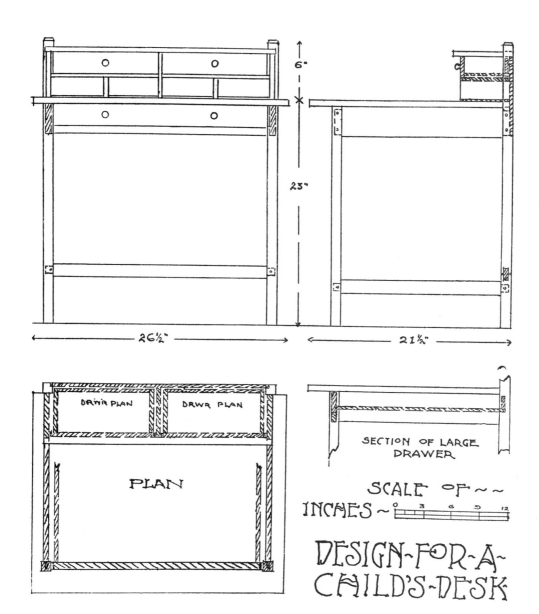

SECTION OF LARGE DRAWER

SCALE OF ~~
INCHES ~ 0   3   6   5   12

DESIGN·FOR·A·
CHILD'S·DESK

Partitions	2	6 in.	2¼ in.	½ in.	2 in.	⅜ in.
Drawer Front	1	24 in.	3¼ in.	⅞ in.	3 in.	¾ in.
Drawer Fronts	2	12 in.	2½ in.	¾ in.	2 in.	½ in.
Drawer Sides	4	6 in.	2¼ in.	½ in.	2 in.	⅜ in.
Drawer Sides	2	19 in.	3¼ in.	¾ in.	3 in.	½ in.
Drawer Backs	2	11 in.	2½ in.	½ in.	2 in.	⅜ in.
Drawer Back	1	22 in.	3 in.	¾ in.	2½ in.	½ in.
Back	1	24 in.	9 in.	¾ in.	8 in.	½ in.

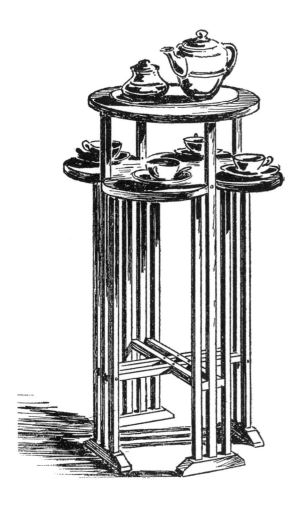

A REALLY convenient little tea table is one of the most useful pieces of furniture in the home sitting-room. And this CRAFTSMAN table model is designed for everyday home use, and is so arranged that the knocking off of cups and saucers as one moves about a room is practically impossible. The upper section is planned to hold tea pot or kettle, with room for sugar bowl and cream pitcher or lemon dish, and the under shelf has detail spaces for each cup and saucer. The effect of the cozy little round spacing for each piece of china is particularly homelike and intimate.

The structural plan for the table is extremely simple, carefully carrying out as it does the strong, plain lines of the CRAFTSMAN idea in furniture. It is not a difficult piece to put together, and should be made to match the color harmony of the room it is used in. It is equally useful for a sewing or reading stand, and if carefully made will become a permanent furniture asset.

MILL BILL OF LUMBER FOR TEA TABLE

Pieces	No.	Long	Rough Wide	Thick	Finish Wide	Thick
Spindles	4	32 in.	7/8 in.	7/8 in.	3/4 in.	3/4 in.
Spindles	8	25 in.	7/8 in.	7/8 in.	3/4 in.	3/4 in.
Top	1	15 in.	15 in.	7/8 in.	15 in. diam.	3/4 in.
Shelf	1	18 in.	18 in.	7/8 in.	Pattern	3/4 in.
Feet	4	7 in.	1½ in.	1¼ in.	1¼ in.	1 in.

DESIGN~FOR~A~TEA~TABLE~

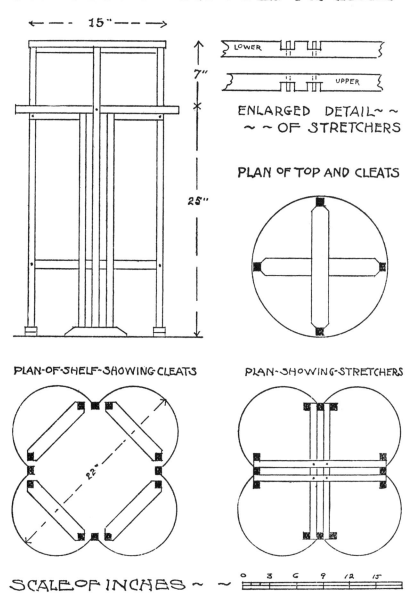

← - - 15" - - →

7"

25"

LOWER

UPPER

ENLARGED DETAIL~ ~
~ ~ OF STRETCHERS

PLAN OF TOP AND CLEATS

PLAN-OF-SHELF~SHOWING-CLEATS

22"

PLAN~SHOWING~STRETCHERS

SCALE OF INCHES ~ ~

0   3   6   9   12   15

Stretchers	. . . .	4	16 in.	1 in.	⅞ in.	⅞ in.	¾ in.
Cleats	. . . .	4	9 in.	2¼ in.	¾ in.	1½ in.	⅝ in.
Cleats	. . . .	2	6 in.	2¼ in.	¾ in.	2 in.	⅝ in.
Cleat	. . . .	1	14 in.	2¼ in.	¾ in.	2 in.	⅝ in.

A COMBINATION ENCYCLOPEDIA TABLE

FOR the student who wishes his reference books as near by as his writing pad, there could be no more valuable piece of furniture than this combination CRAFTSMAN table and encyclopedia bookcase. It is thoughtfully designed to hold a complete set of books, with additional space for dictionary. Or, of course, it could be used for any number of other sorts of reference books, dictionaries, etc., in fact, for whatever books the student wishes to surround himself with.

This model is one of the plainest CRAFTSMAN designs, most substantially made to hold the heaviest of books and to last a lifetime. The working plans are so simple that they can be understood and applied by the beginner in cabinet work. And what recreation could a student enjoy more thoroughly than to become his own cabinetmaker and to develop a table on which he is to work. This model is recommended as one of the most practical, substantial, and simple of our series of lessons in cabinet work.

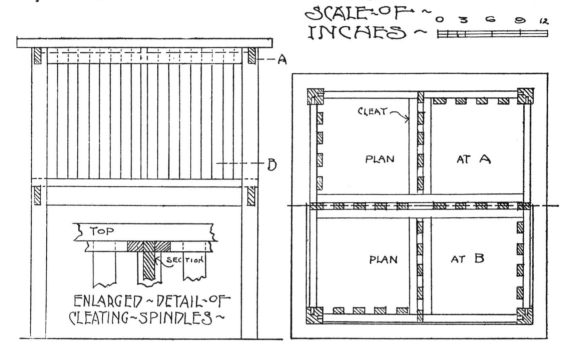

DESIGN~OF~A~COMBINATION~TABLE~
AND~BOOK~CASE~FOR~ENCYCLOPÆDIA~

SCALE~OF~ 0 3 6 9 12
INCHES ~

A

B

TOP

SECTION

ENLARGED ~ DETAIL~OF~
CLEATING~SPINDLES ~

CLEAT~

PLAN   AT A

PLAN   AT B

MILL BILL OF LUMBER FOR COMBINATION TABLE AND ENCYCLO-
PEDIA BOOKCASE.

				Rough		Finish	
Pieces	No.	Long	Wide	Thick		Wide	Thick
Legs	4	31 in.	2 in.	2 in.		$1\frac{3}{4}$ in.	$1\frac{3}{4}$ in.
Top	1	28 in.	28 in.	1 in.		27 in.	$\frac{7}{8}$ in.
Shelf	1	25 in.	25 in.	$\frac{7}{8}$ in.		24 in.	$\frac{3}{4}$ in.
Rails	8	23 in.	$2\frac{1}{4}$ in.	1 in.		2 in.	$\frac{7}{8}$ in.
Slats	36	15 in.	$1\frac{1}{4}$ in.	$\frac{5}{8}$ in.		1 in.	$\frac{1}{2}$ in.
Cleats	4	11 in.	$1\frac{1}{4}$ in.	$\frac{3}{4}$ in.		1 in.	$\frac{5}{8}$ in.
Cleats	2	24 in.	$1\frac{1}{4}$ in.	$\frac{3}{4}$ in.		1 in.	$\frac{5}{8}$ in.

A HALL MIRROR

ONE piece of furniture that is well-nigh indispensable in a hall is the mirror. The model shown here, like the rest of the hall furniture, is plain to severity in design, all its charm depending on the nicety of proportion and workmanship. The corners show the same mortise and tenon construction, with the tenons projecting slightly and very carefully finished. The top of the frame

shows a very slight curve,—so slight that it is hardly preceptible, yet it makes all the difference between an effect of crudity and one of carefully designed proportions. The chains from which the mirror hangs should be of wrought iron, with fairly heavy links. The hat hooks on the sides of the mirror may be of iron, brass or copper, according to the tone of the wood and the general color scheme of the room.

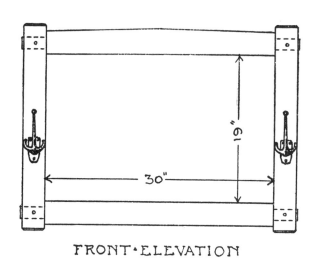

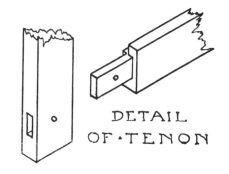

FRONT·ELEVATION

SECTION

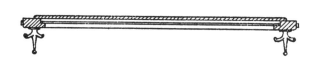

HORIZONTAL·SECTION

DETAIL
OF·TENON

DESIGN
FOR·A·HALL·MIRROR

SCALE·OF·INCHES

MILL BILL OF LUMBER FOR HALL MIRROR

Pieces.	No.	ROUGH.			FINISHED.	
		Long.	Wide.	Thick.	Wide.	Thick.
Top rail.......	1	37 in.	4 in.	1¼ in.	3½ in.	1⅛ in.
Lower rail.....	1	37 in.	3½ in.	1¼ in.	3 in.	1⅛ in.
Stiles	2	27 in.	3½ in.	1¼ in.	3 in.	1⅛ in.
Back	1	34 in.	23 in.	¼ in.		

A LIBRARY TABLE.

THIS generously proportioned table, with its ample top and sturdy structure, is especially fitted for use in a library, where a table with plenty of room for the books, magazines, and newspapers that one may be using is well-nigh indispensable. It is massive in construction, but not clumsy, owing to the curved lines and open spaces which soften the severity of the solid ends and the keys and tenons which form an effective structural decoration. A brace beneath the top keeps the ends firm, and the lower shelf acts as another brace.

MILL BILL OF STOCK FOR LIBRARY TABLE.

Pieces.	No.	Long	Rough. Wide	Thick	Finished. Wide	Thick
Top	1	73 in.	37 in.	1⅜ in.	36 in.	1¼ in.
Sides	2	27½ in.	27½ in.	1⅜ in.	pattern	1¼ in.
Braces	3	25 in.	2 in.	1¾ in.	1¾ in.	1½ in.
Shelf	1	62 in.	12½ in.	1⅛ in.	12 in.	1 in.

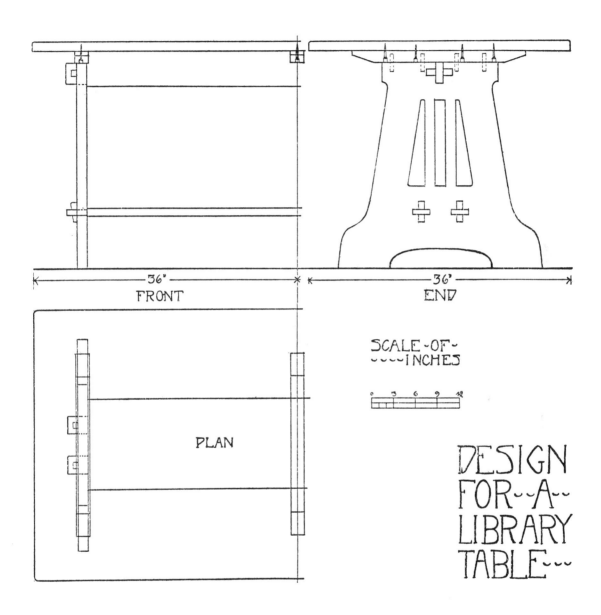

36"

FRONT

36"

END

PLAN

SCALE ·OF·
· · · INCHES

0   3   6   9   12

DESIGN
FOR··A··
LIBRARY
TABLE···

CRAFTSMAN HALL TREE

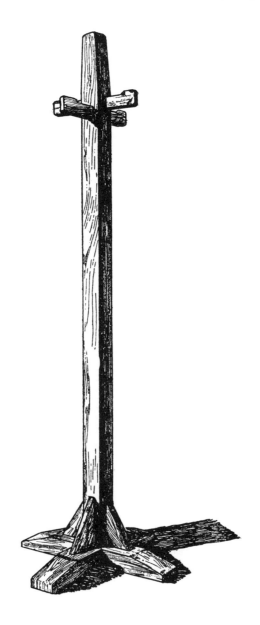

HALL furniture has been selected for this number of the cabinet work series for the reason that it seems harder to procure really simple and satisfactory furnishings for the hall than for any other part of the house. The model shown here can easily be made at home by anyone at all skilled in the use of tools. The convenience of a simple hall tree of this design is that it takes up so little room, and yet affords accommodation for a good many coats. It will stand in any nook or corner out of the way, which is more than can be said of the larger and more elaborate trees that sometimes appear to take up nearly all the room there is in the hall. This design is simple to a degree, but must be very carefully made and finished in order to produce the best effect. As will be seen by careful study of the details, crudity is not sought, either in shape or workmanship. The pole must be very delicately tapered at the top in order to avoid clumsiness, and the mortising must be very carefully done, if the piece is to have the craftsman-like appearance that constitutes its chief claim to beauty.

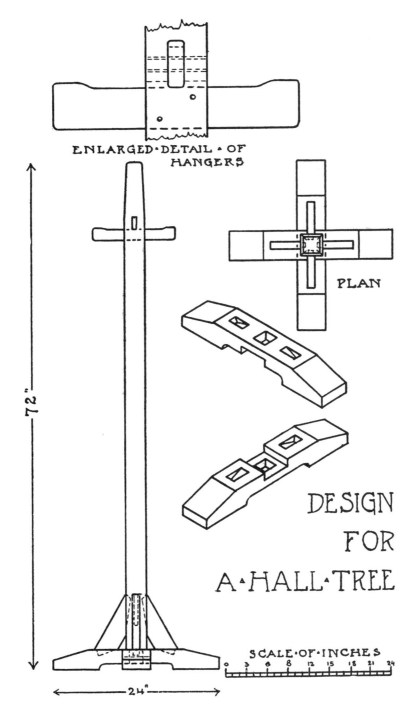

ENLARGED·DETAIL·OF HANGERS

PLAN

DESIGN
FOR
A·HALL·TREE

SCALE·OF·INCHES

MILL BILL OF LUMBER FOR HALL TREE

		Rough.			Finished.	
Pieces.	No.	Long.	Wide.	Thick.	Wide.	Thick.
Post	1	72 in.	4 in.	4 in.	3 in.	3 in.
Feet	2	24 in.	4½ in.	3 in.	4 in.	2¾ in.
Braces	4	10 in.	4 in.	1¼ in.	3 in.	1⅛ in.
Hangers	2	12 in.	2 in.	⅞ in.	1¾ in.	¾ in.

THIS model for a bookcase has two drawers below for papers or magazines, and three adjustable shelves that can be moved to any height desired, simply by changing the position of the pegs that support the shelves. If the books are small, an additional shelf might be put in if required. The frame of the bookcase is perfectly plain, the smooth surface of the sides being broken only by the tenons of the top and bottom. The general effect is straight and square, but the very slight curve at the top of both back and sides takes away any appearance of crudity.

MILL BILL OF LUMBER FOR BOOKCASE

Pieces	No.	Long	Rough Wide	Rough Thick	Finished Wide	Finished Thick
Sides	2	67 in.	17 in.	1 in.	16½ in.	⅞ in.
Top and shelves....	3	38½ in.	16 in.	1 in.	15⅜ in.	⅞ in.
Top of back.......	1	37 in.	7 in.	1 in.	6 in.	⅞ in.
Bottom of back....	1	37 in.	12 in.	1 in.	11½ in.	⅞ in.
Back side stiles....	2	50¼ in.	4 in.	1 in.	3½ in.	⅞ in.
Back center stile...	1	50¼ in.	4 in.	1 in.	3½ in.	⅞ in.

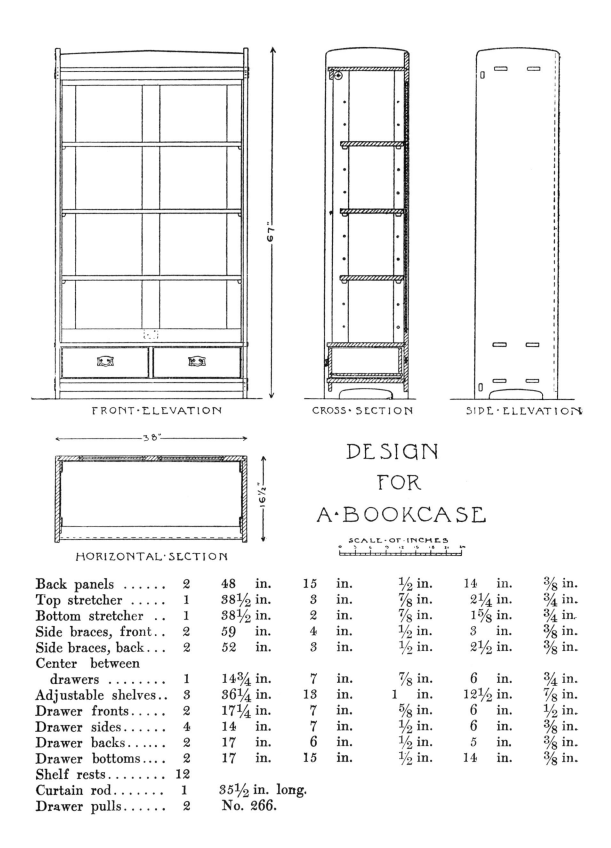

FRONT·ELEVATION   CROSS·SECTION   SIDE·ELEVATION

HORIZONTAL·SECTION

DESIGN
FOR
A·BOOKCASE

SCALE·OF·INCHES

Back panels	2	48 in.	15 in.	½ in.	14 in.	⅜ in.
Top stretcher	1	38½ in.	3 in.	⅞ in.	2¼ in.	¾ in.
Bottom stretcher ..	1	38½ in.	2 in.	⅞ in.	1⅝ in.	¾ in.
Side braces, front..	2	59 in.	4 in.	½ in.	3 in.	⅜ in.
Side braces, back...	2	52 in.	3 in.	½ in.	2½ in.	⅜ in.
Center between drawers	1	14¾ in.	7 in.	⅞ in.	6 in.	¾ in.
Adjustable shelves..	3	36¼ in.	13 in.	1 in.	12½ in.	⅞ in.
Drawer fronts.....	2	17¼ in.	7 in.	⅝ in.	6 in.	½ in.
Drawer sides......	4	14 in.	7 in.	½ in.	6 in.	⅜ in.
Drawer backs......	2	17 in.	6 in.	½ in.	5 in.	⅜ in.
Drawer bottoms....	2	17 in.	15 in.	½ in.	14 in.	⅜ in.
Shelf rests........	12					
Curtain rod.......	1	35½ in. long.				
Drawer pulls......	2	No. 266.				

A CRAFTSMAN WOOD-BOX

THIS heavily constructed wood-box is designed to serve for a seat as well. The framework is solid and massive, with square corner posts, into which the side and end pieces are mortised. The boards, of which the sides, top and ends are made, are V-jointed and spliced together to prevent spreading in case the heat of the fire should cause them to shrink. The back is rather higher than the sides, and affords a support for pillows, while the front is carefully leveled off, so that no ridge of framework interferes with the comfort of the seat.

MILL BILL OF LUMBER FOR WOOD BOX

Pieces	No.	Long	Rough			Finished	
			Wide	Thick		Wide	Thick
Posts, front	2	22 in.	4 in.	4 in.		3 in.	3 in.
Posts, back	2	25 in.	4 in.	4 in.		3 in.	3 in.
Front and back stretchers	4	60½ in.	4 in.	1¼ in.		3½ in.	1⅛ in.
Side stretchers	4	30½ in.	3½ in.	1¼ in.		3 in.	1⅛ in.
*Back panel	1	55½ in.	18 in.	⅞ in.		17 in.	¾ in.

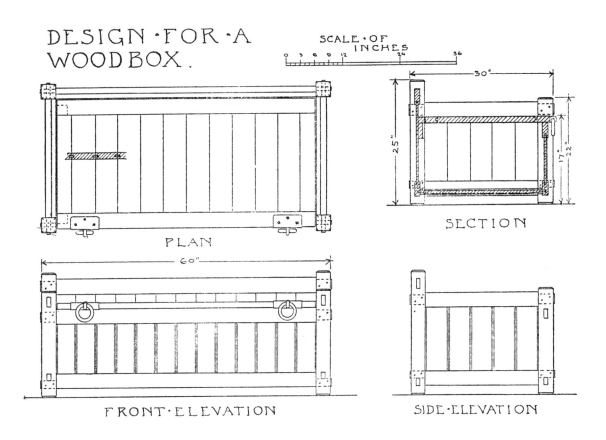

DESIGN·FOR·A WOODBOX.

SCALE·OF INCHES

PLAN

SECTION

FRONT·ELEVATION

SIDE·ELEVATION

*Front panel	1	55½ in.	12	in.	⅞ in.	10	in.	¾ in.
*Side panels	2	25½ in.	15	in.	⅞ in.	14½	in.	¾ in.
Side rails	2	24 in.	1	in.	1 in.	15/16	in.	⅞ in.
Back rails	1	54 in.	1	in.	1 in.	15/16	in.	⅞ in.
Support	1	55½ in.	3	in.	1 in.	2½	in.	⅞ in.
Bottom	1	56½ in.	28	in.	1 in.	27	in.	⅞ in.
Bottom support ...	2	27 in.	4	in.	1¼ in.	3½	in.	1⅛ in.
Top stiles	2	54 in.	4	in.	1 in.	3	in.	⅞ in.
Top rails	2	24 in.	4	in.	1 in.	3	in.	⅞ in.
Top panel	1	48 in.	20	in.	1 in.	18	in.	⅞ in.
Strips...........		70 feet.						
Hinges..........	2 pairs.							
Lifting handles....	2							

*V-jointed.

SECRETAIRE

THIS is a piece which will require careful work, good joints and the use of well seasoned wood. The legs, caps, bases and feet can be turned at a very small expense at almost any wood working shop. These are fastened with half-inch dowels, three being used in each leg. The lid is veneered on both sides, the grain of the core running across, and the outside and inside, up and down. This is done so as to avoid warping. The pulls for the drawer may be of metal or wood and are turned in a quaint old fashioned shape. The lid is held by a pair of support hinges which are always to be had in brass. The hinges are ordinary butts, 2 inches x 2½ inches when open.

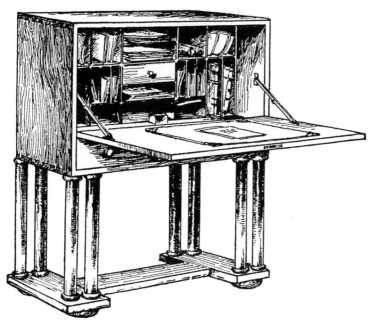

MILL BILL FOR SECRETAIRE

Pieces	No.	Long	ROUGH Wide	Thick	FINISH Wide	Thick	Wood
Top and bottom shelf	3	38 in.	16½ in.	1 in.	16 in.	¾ in.	oak
Sides	2	25 in.	16½ in.	1 in.	16 in.	¾ in.	oak
Base	1	28 in.	6¼ in.	1½ in.	6 in.	1⅜ in.	oak
Base	2	18 in.	7 in.	1½ in.	6¾ in.	1⅜ in.	oak
Back	1	36 in.	24 in.	¾ in.	23½ in.	½ in.	oak
Lid	1	36 in.	17¼ in.	¾ in.	17 in.	⅝ in.	oak
Veneer for lid	2	17 in.	36 in.	1/16 in.	..	..	
Stop	1	36 in.	¾ in.	1 in.	½ in.	⅞ in.	oak
Legs	8	19 in.	2¼ in.	2¼ in.	2 in.	turned	oak
Base and caps	8	1¼ in.	3¼ in.	3¼ in.	3 in.	turned	oak
Feet	4	2 in.	5¼ in.	5¼ in.	5 in.	turned	oak
Drawer front	1	35 in.	4¼ in.	1 in.	4 in.	⅞ in.	oak
Drawer back	1	35 in.	4 in.	¾ in.	3¾ in.	½ in.	oak
Drawer sides	1	16 in.	4¼ in.	¾ in.	4 in.	½ in.	oak
Drawer bottom	1	35 in.	16 in.	¼ in.	15½ in.	½ in.	oak
Interior							Red cedar
Top, bottom, center	3	35 in.	10¼ in.	⅜ in.	10 in.	¼ in.	"
Side and center	4	18 in.	10¼ in.	⅜ in.	10 in.	¼ in.	"
Drawer front	1	10 in.	3¼ in.	⅞ in.	3 in.	¾ in.	"
Partitions		16 running feet			11 in.	⅛ in.	"

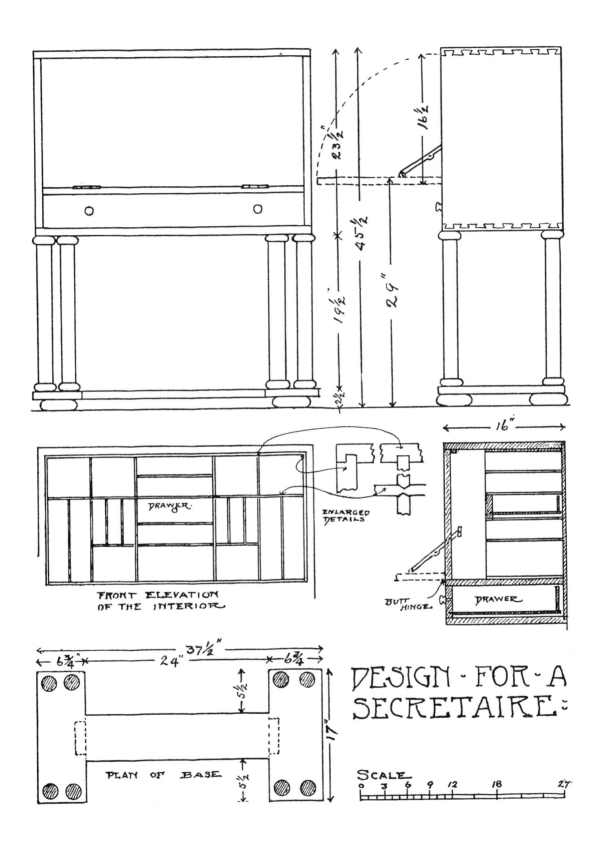

DRAWER.

ENLARGED
DETAILS

FRONT ELEVATION
OF THE INTERIOR

BUTT
HINGE

DRAWER

PLAN OF BASE

DESIGN · FOR · A
SECRETAIRE ·

SCALE
0 3 6 9 12   18   27

109

CRAFTSMAN LEATHER-COVERED STOOL

IN the designs for home cabinet work published this month we have some-what changed the models, showing forms that are a slight departure from the severity of the CRAFTSMAN style. As will be seen by a glance at the illustrations showing the finished pieces, they are rather more massive in appearance than those we have been giving heretofore. This is because these designs are intended primarily to be carried out in cypress, chestnut, California redwood or similar woods, where the softness of texture and com-

parative lightness in weight admit the use of apparently a more massive con-struction than does a hard, heavy wood like the oak. Many people interested in home cabinet making live in parts of the country where these softer woods are much more easily obtainable and less expensive than the oak, and it is for these workers that the present designs are intended, although, of course, they would serve admirably for oak if the maker did not mind considerable weight in the piece.

A departure from the absolutely straight lines of most of the CRAFTSMAN models is made in these designs, and most workers will find in them a new element of suggestiveness for development along lines of original design, which is most desirable in any form of home handicraft. As given here the models are severely plain, but to the worker who is developing a perception of legiti-

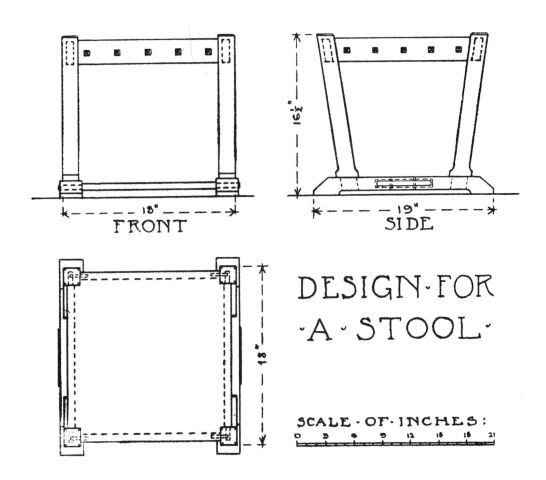

FRONT   SIDE

DESIGN·FOR
·A·STOOL·

SCALE·OF·INCHES:

MILL BILL OF STOCK FOR STOOL

Pieces	No.	Long	Rough		Finished	
			Wide	Thick	Wide	Thick
Legs....................	4	17 in.	2½ in.	2 in.	pattern	1¾ in.
Feet....................	2	19 in.	2½ in.	1⅞ in.	2¼ in.	pattern
Crosspiece..............	1	19 in.	6 in.	1 in.	5¾ in.	⅞ in.
Seat Rails...............	4	18 in.	2½ in.	1 in.	2¼ in.	⅞ in.
Sole Leather for Seat.......	1	27 in.	27 in.			

mate decoration as applied to wood-working they will be found particularly suggestive in the scope they afford for structural ornamentation.

While any wood suitable for cabinet work may be used for these pieces, we have suggested the three already mentioned as being especially effective when used for forms of this character. The cypress has such prominent markings that large surfaces are necessary to show them to advantage, and it is so coarse in grain that any slenderness would give a suggestion of weakness.

The same applies to chestnut and even more strongly to the redwood, which is so largely used in California both for the interior woodwork of houses and for all sorts of home-wrought furniture.

A close study of the stool shown as the first model will reveal the leading structural characteristics of all three pieces. The appearance of crudity that might be given by the massiveness of construction is softened by the fine finish that should appear in every detail. In the posts all the edges should be slightly rounded, suggesting heavy hewn timbers, and the corners should be carefully chamfered so that all appearance of the crude edge of sawn lumber is avoided. Any clumsiness at the bottom is obviated by the curving out of the posts, and by beveling the end pieces. The crosspiece is mortised firmly into these end pieces, the projecting tenons forming a slight touch of decoration, and the whole structure is firmly pinned together. The seat must be made with special care to preserve the fine straight lines and flat top. A

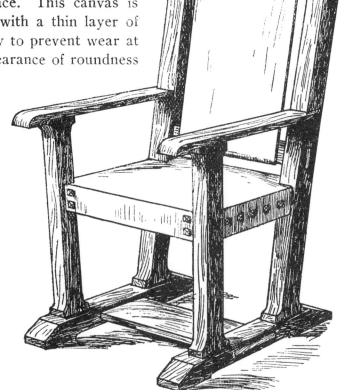

piece of heavy canvas should first be stretched over the seat rails, wrapped clear around and nailed far up on the under side to assure a firm and evenly stretched surface. This canvas is to be covered on the top with a thin layer of cotton, which serves merely to prevent wear at the edge and gives no appearance of roundness or of padding. The seat covering is of sole leather. This should be dampened on the under side to render it flexible and then carefully stretched by hand, wrapped around and nailed firmly underneath. As it dries all wrinkles and unevenness will be shrunk out of the leather, leaving a perfectly smooth and even surface. Large square-headed nails of wrought iron are placed at regular intervals on the outside of the rails and serve as an additional stay to the leather as well as a decoration.

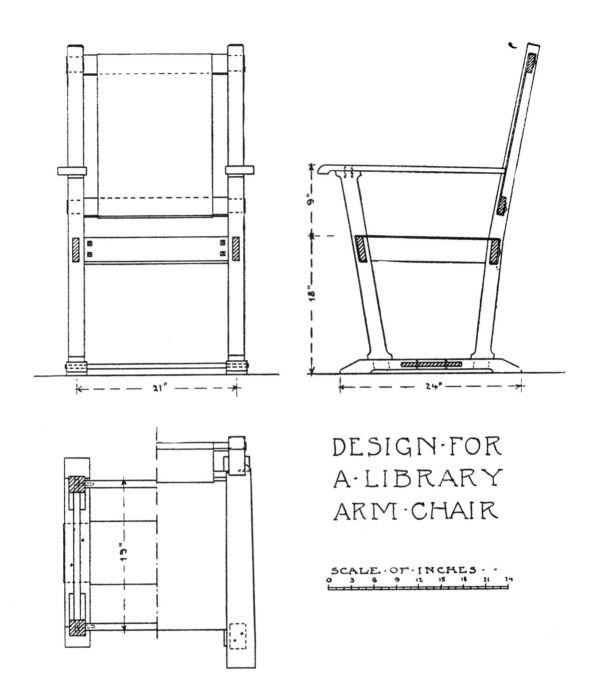

DESIGN·FOR
A·LIBRARY
ARM·CHAIR

SCALE·OF·INCHES··
0 3 6 9 12 15 18 21 24

MILL BILL OF STOCK FOR ARMCHAIR

Pieces	No.	Long	Rough		Finished	
			Wide	Thick	Wide	Thick
Front Legs	2	27 in.	3½ in.	2½ in.	pattern	2 in.
Back Legs	2	42 in.	4½ in.	2½ in.	pattern	2 in.
Feet	2	24 in.	3 in.	2 in.	2⅝ in.	pattern
Crosspiece	1	24 in.	8 in.	1 in.	7½ in.	⅞ in.
Arms	2	27 in.	4 in.	1½ in.	3¾ in.	pattern
Seat Rails	4	21 in.	3¼ in.	1 in.	3 in.	⅞ in.
Back Slats	2	23 in.	2½ in.	1 in.	2½ in.	⅞ in.
Sole Leather for Back	1	27 in.	15 in.			
Sole Leather for Seat	1	30 in.	27 in.			

The chair is simply a further development of the same form of construction that obtains in the stool. The structure at the bottom is precisely the same. The arms should be very carefully and symmetrically rounded at the ends, both to give a finished and workmanlike look to the piece and to afford a better grasp for the hands in rising. The mortise and tenon construction, all carefully pinned with wooden pins, prevails throughout, and the sole leather seat is made in the same way as that of the stool. The back of the chair is made of a single piece of sole leather, stretched on and wrapped clear around the rails at the top and bottom.

The construction of the table is another development of the form shown in the chair and stool, and here the inward slope of the legs is even more pronounced than in the chair. While very massive in appearance, the table, if made of one of the woods suggested, will not in reality be as heavy as it looks. Were it made of oak it would be practically a stationary piece, as the chances are that it would be too heavy to move. This table is very firmly built with the mortise and tenon construction, and the only touch of decoration, aside from the tenons, appears in the use of the large wooden pins that hold the piece together. The rounded edges and curved lines that appear in the structure of the lower part give a feeling of the use of massive timbers without any repellent impression of clumsiness, and with reasonably careful workman-

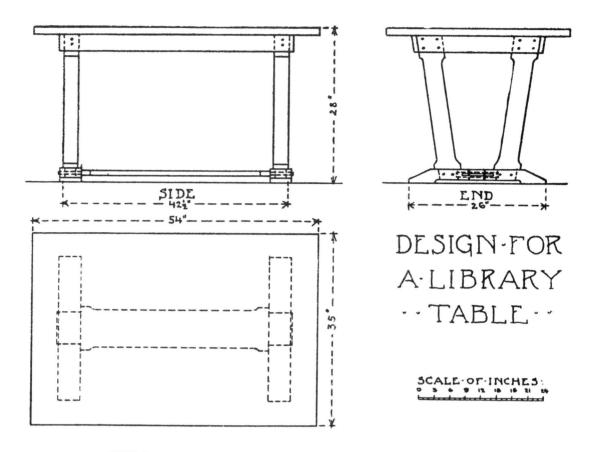

SIDE
42½"

54"

35"

28"

END
26"

DESIGN·FOR
A·LIBRARY
··TABLE··

SCALE·OF·INCHES
0 3 6 9 12 15 18 21 24

MILL BILL OF STOCK FOR LIBRARY TABLE

| Pieces | No. | Long | Rough | | | Finished | |
			Wide	Thick	Wide	Thick
Top	1	54½ in.	35½ in.	1¾ in.	32 in.	1½ in.
Legs	4	28 in.	5 in.	3 in.	pattern	2¾ in.
Feet	2	26½ in.	4 in.	2½ in.	3¾ in.	pattern
Crosspiece	1	44 in.	8½ in.	1¼ in.	pattern	1 in.
Side Rims	2	45 in.	3½ in.	1 in.	3 in.	⅞ in.
End Rims	2	25 in.	3½ in.	1 in.	3 in.	⅞ in.

ship the piece should have a most attractive quality. The top, of course, should be finished with great care, which must first of all be exercised in the selection of particularly choice wood for the large plain surface where the grain shows so prominently.

115

A FOLDING CARD TABLE.

T HE little folding table shown here is designed primarily for a card
table, but it is useful for anything where a small stand is required.
With one or both of the leaves down it makes a capital little table
to stand against the wall for a jardinière, or for anything that requires
the background of the wall, and with the round top it makes a good stand
anywhere in the room and can be used for a tea table or a sewing table as
well as for cards. The lower structure is somewhat massive in form and
very severe in outline, but if well made and pinned together with wooden
pins, as shown in the illustration, there is a decorative quality in the very
uncompromising straightness of it. The top, of course, should be made of
selected wood and very carefully finished; in fact, careful workmanship is
especially essential in as plain a piece as this, for without satin-smooth
surface and carefully softened edges and corners it could easily be made to
look very crude and unattractive.

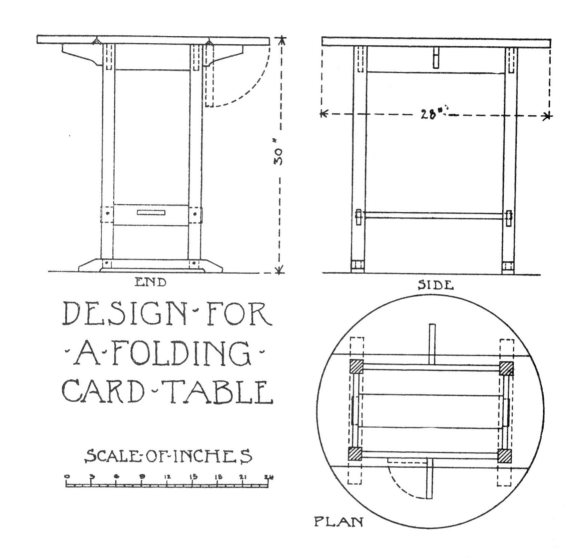

END

SIDE

28"

30"

DESIGN·FOR
·A·FOLDING·
CARD·TABLE

SCALE·OF·INCHES

PLAN

MILL BILL OF STOCK FOR A FOLDING CARD TABLE

Pieces	No.	Long	Rough		Finished	
			Wide	Thick	Wide	Thick
Legs	4	29 in.	$1\frac{3}{4}$ in.	$1\frac{3}{4}$ in.	$1\frac{5}{8}$ in.	$1\frac{5}{8}$ in.
Feet	2	18 id.	$1\frac{3}{4}$ in.	$1\frac{1}{4}$ in.	$1\frac{5}{8}$ in.	pattern
Side Rims	2	22 in.	4 in.	$\frac{7}{8}$ in.	$3\frac{1}{4}$ in.	$\frac{3}{4}$ in.
End Rims	2	11 in.	4 in.	$\frac{7}{8}$ in.	$3\frac{1}{2}$ in.	$\frac{3}{4}$ in.
Brackets	2	$5\frac{1}{2}$ in.	3 in.	$\frac{3}{4}$ in.	pattern	$\frac{5}{8}$ in.
End Stretchers	2	13 in.	3 in.	$1\frac{1}{4}$ in.	$2\frac{1}{2}$ in.	1 in.
Shelf	1	20 in.	$4\frac{1}{2}$ in.	$\frac{7}{8}$ in.	4 in.	$\frac{3}{4}$ in.
Top Center	1	30 in.	14 in.	$\frac{7}{8}$ in.	$13\frac{1}{2}$ in.	$\frac{3}{4}$ in.
Top Sides	2	25 in.	8 in.	$\frac{7}{8}$ in.	$7\frac{1}{2}$ in.	$\frac{3}{4}$ in.

A BOOKCASE AND CUPBOARD.

MILL BILL OF STOCK FOR BOOK CASE.

	No.	Long.	Rough. Wide.	Rough. Thick.	Finished. Wide.	Finished. Thick.
Top	1	52 in.	14 in.	1 in.	13½ in.	⅞ in.
Sides	2	39 in.	13 in.	1 in.	12 in.	⅞ in.
Center shelves...	3	23⅞ in.	10½ in.	⅞ in.	9½ in.	¾ in.
Side shelves.....	6	10½ in.	10½ in.	⅞ in.	9½ in.	¾ in.
Bottom shelf.....	1	46 in.	12½ in.	1 in.	12 in.	⅞ in.
SIDE DOORS—						
Top rails........	2	9 in.	2¼ in.	1 in.	2 in.	⅞ in.
Bottom rails.....	2	9 in.	3¼ in.	1 in.	3 in.	⅞ in.
Stiles	4	35½ in.	2⅛ in.	1 in.	1⅞ in.	⅞ in.
Mullions	2	32 in.	1¼ in.	1⅛ in.	⅞ in.	1 in.
Mullions	14	37¼ in.	1¼ in.	1⅛ in.	⅞ in.	1 in.
Cathedral Glass..	32	3¼ in.	3¼ in.			
PANEL DOORS—						
Top rails........	2	10 in.	2¾ in.	1 in.	2½ in.	⅞ in.
Bottom rails.....	2	10 in.	3¼ in.	1 in.	3 in.	⅞ in.
Stiles...........	4	25½ in.	2¾ in.	1 in.	2½ in.	⅞ in.
Panels	2	21 in.	8½ in.	½ in.	8¼ in.	⅜ in.
Top panel.......	1	20½ in.	6¾ in.	½ in.	6½ in.	⅜ in.

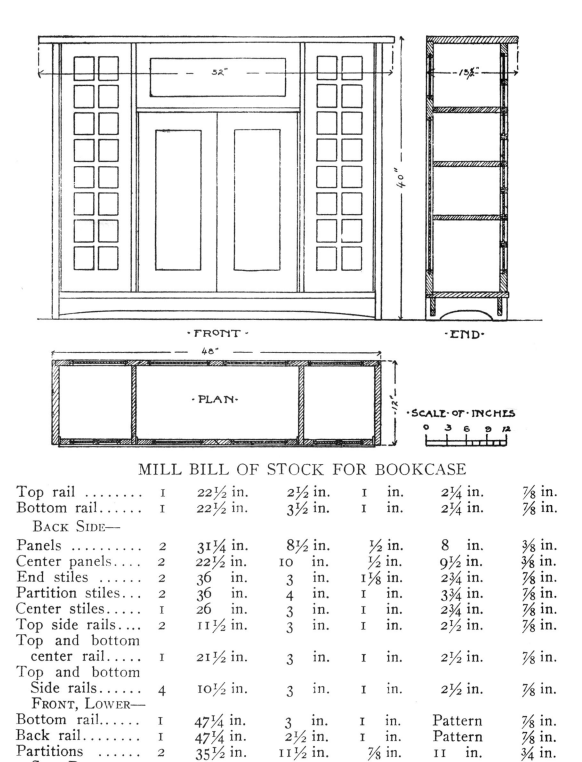

·FRONT·   ·END·

·PLAN·

·SCALE·OF·INCHES·
0 3 6 9 12

MILL BILL OF STOCK FOR BOOKCASE

Top rail	1	22½ in.	2½ in.	1 in.	2¼ in.	⅞ in.
Bottom rail......	1	22½ in.	3½ in.	1 in.	2¼ in.	⅞ in.
BACK SIDE—						
Panels	2	31¼ in.	8½ in.	½ in.	8 in.	⅜ in.
Center panels....	2	22½ in.	10 in.	½ in.	9½ in.	⅜ in.
End stiles	2	36 in.	3 in.	1⅛ in.	2¾ in.	⅞ in.
Partition stiles...	2	36 in.	4 in.	1 in.	3¾ in.	⅞ in.
Center stiles.....	1	26 in.	3 in.	1 in.	2¾ in.	⅞ in.
Top side rails....	2	11½ in.	3 in.	1 in.	2½ in.	⅞ in.
Top and bottom center rail.....	1	21½ in.	3 in.	1 in.	2½ in.	⅞ in.
Top and bottom Side rails......	4	10½ in.	3 in.	1 in.	2½ in.	⅞ in.
FRONT, LOWER—						
Bottom rail......	1	47¼ in.	3 in.	1 in.	Pattern	⅞ in.
Back rail........	1	47¼ in.	2½ in.	1 in.	Pattern	⅞ in.
Partitions	2	35½ in.	11½ in.	⅞ in.	11 in.	¾ in.
SIDE DOOR—						
Stops	2	35½ in.	1½ in.	⅝ in.	1¼ in.	½ in.
Stops	2	25½ in.	1½ in.	⅝ in.	1¼ in.	½ in.

Index of Projects